MONEY SMARTS

THE GUIDE TO

INVESTING IN MUTUAL FUNDS

HOW TO B·U·I·L·D YOUR WEALTH BY MASTERING THE BASIC STRATEGIES

Other Money Smarts Titles
by David L. Scott
from the Globe Pequot Press

The Guide to Personal Budgeting

The Guide to Investing in Common Stocks

The Guide to Investing in Bonds

The Guide to Buying Insurance

The Guide to Managing Credit

The Guide to Tax-Saving Investing

The Guide to Investing for Current Income

The Guide to Saving Money

Also by David L. Scott

Dictionary of Accounting

Fundamentals of the Time Value of Money

How Wall Street Works: The Basics and Beyond

Investing in Tax-Saving Municipal Bonds

The Investor's Guide to Discount Brokers

Municipal Bonds: The Basics and Beyond

Security Investments

Understanding and Managing Investment Risk and Return

Wall Street Words

MONEY SMARTS

THE GUIDE TO INVESTING IN MUTUAL FUNDS

HOW TO B•U•I•L•D YOUR WEALTH BY MASTERING THE BASIC STRATEGIES

All New Second Edition

by David L. Scott

The Globe Pequot Press

OLD SAYBROOK, CONNECTICUT

This book's purpose is to provide accurate and authoritative information on the topics covered. It is sold with the understanding that neither the author nor the publisher is engaged in rendering legal, financial, accounting, or other professional services. Neither the Globe Pequot Press nor the author assumes any liability resulting from action taken based on the information included herein. Mention of a company name does not constitute endorsement.

Library of Congress Cataloging-in-Publication Data

Scott, David Logan, 1942-
The guide to investing in mutual funds : how to build your wealth by mastering the basic strategies / by David L. Scott. -- 2nd ed.
p. cm. -- (Money smarts)
Includes index.
ISBN 1-56440-879-5
1. Mutual funds. I. Title. II. Series: Scott, David Logan, 1942–Money smarts.
HG4530.S39 1996
332.63'27--dc20 96-12941
CIP

Figure on page 149 courtesy of Value Line Mutual Fund Survey; figure on page 150 courtesy of Arthur Wiesenberger Services; figure on page 151 courtesy of Morningstar, Inc.

Manufactured in the United States of America
Second Edition/First Printing

Contents

Introduction

Perhaps you are considering an investment in a mutual fund but hesitate because you don't fully understand how mutual funds would use your money to earn a return. You may consider a mutual fund to be a risky investment even though you aren't sure why. Perhaps you would like to buy shares of a mutual fund but are uncertain what type of mutual fund you should purchase. Maybe you have already invested in a mutual fund even though you didn't understand exactly what you were buying at the time. Perhaps you still don't. If you find yourself in any of these situations, or if you just plain don't understand what mutual funds do with investors' money, this book is for you. *The Guide to Investing in Mutual Funds* covers the essentials of mutual funds for people who don't have much knowledge of these popular investments. Included in this book is information concerning:

- how mutual funds are organized and brought to market;
- what kinds of income you can expect to earn if you invest in mutual funds;
- how to buy and sell shares of mutual funds;
- the differences between stock funds and bond funds;
- the importance of a mutual fund's investment objective;
- how to select a mutual fund;
- how to save on fees when you buy or redeem shares of a mutual fund;
- investment alternatives to mutual funds;
- where to search for information about mutual funds.

Mutual funds are not particularly difficult to understand, especially when you have some knowledge about the common stocks and bonds that these investment companies own. Those of you who need to brush up a little on these securities will find basic information on stocks and bonds in Chapters 3 and 4. The better you understand these investments, the more likely you are to choose a fund that best serves your investment needs. If you feel you need more basic information about stocks and bonds, consider picking up copies of *The Guide to Investing in Common Stocks* and *The Guide to Investing in Bonds*, two other titles in this Money Smarts series.

To invest in a mutual fund, you need to know more than just where to send your check. Mutual funds are offered in many varieties, from the ultrasafe to the very risky. The shares of some mutual funds are subject to wide fluctuations in value, which can cause you to suffer substantial losses, especially if you need to sell your shares on relatively short notice. Other mutual funds virtually guarantee that you can sell your shares for the price you paid.

You may feel the professional managers employed by a mutual fund should be able to solve most of your investment problems. After all, how can you go wrong when well-paid, high-powered financial advisers are managing the mutual fund's investments? Shouldn't you be able to rely on the financial managers to take care of investing your money to maximum advantage? In truth, even a well-managed mutual fund may turn out to be a poor investment choice if the fund's investment objective is not consistent with your own investment goals.

David L. Scott
Valdosta, Georgia

CHAPTER 1

An Introduction to Mutual Funds

A mutual fund is a financial organization that uses funds invested by the shareholders to acquire a portfolio of securities that is managed for the benefit of the owners. Mutual funds have a unique corporate structure that permits investors to redeem shares at any time directly through the company. Shareholders of a mutual fund earn a return on their investment from dividends and capital gains that are earned and distributed by the fund, and from possible increases in the market values of the shares they own. Mutual funds are attractive investment alternatives for individuals who want to gain access to diversified and professionally managed portfolios of securities.

Mutual funds have become one of America's favorite investments. From a mid-1920s introduction in the United States, the mutual fund industry has expanded until there are now approximately 6,000 different funds that manage assets worth more than $2.2 trillion. Whether you are interested in investing your money in bonds, stocks, or a combination of the two, you may be able to invest more profitably, more safely, and less expensively by investing in mutual funds rather than purchasing securities directly.

Thousands of different mutual funds offer virtually any type of diversified or specialized stock or bond portfolio you desire. Many mutual funds specialize in owning the common stocks of growth companies while other mutual funds invest primarily in stocks that pay a high dividend return. An increasing number of mutual funds have a narrow focus and invest only in the stocks of companies that operate in particular industries or companies that concentrate their operations in particular countries or regions of the world. Still other mutual funds invest only in specific types of fixed-income debt such as bonds that have long maturities, high-risk bonds, or bonds that pay tax-exempt interest. Some mutual funds even restrict their investments to tax-exempt bonds that have been issued in a particular state.

The Fundamentals of Mutual Funds

A mutual fund is a type of investment company that invests its owners' money in financial securities. Manufacturing and service companies—such as Amoco, Coca-Cola, General Electric, and Apple Computer—use the capital contributed by their owners to pay for equipment, land, buildings, and

Figure 1

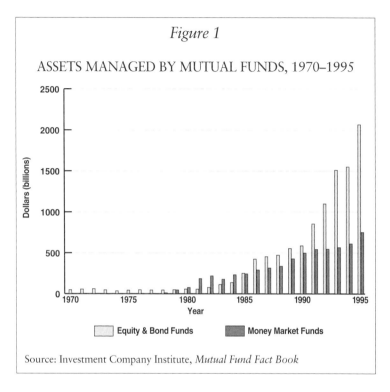

ASSETS MANAGED BY MUTUAL FUNDS, 1970–1995

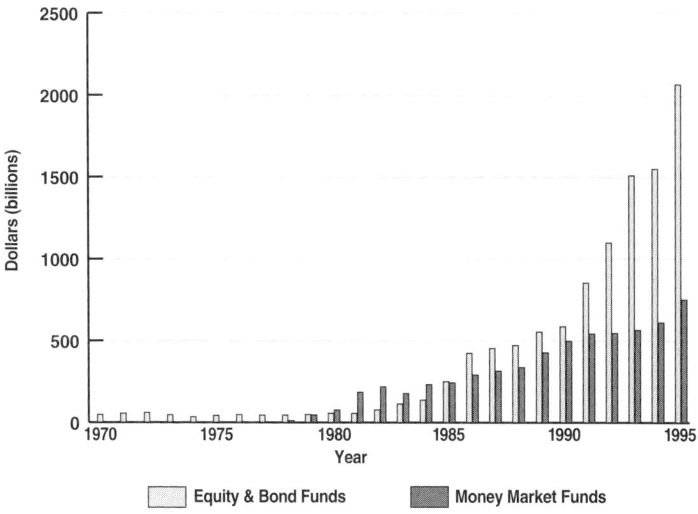

Source: Investment Company Institute, *Mutual Fund Fact Book*

production materials used to produce goods or services that are sold to earn a profit for the owners. Rather than buy assets that can be used to make things or do things, mutual funds use stockholder capital to buy stocks, bonds, and money market securities for the benefit of the funds' owners. And while most companies serve customers who are distinct from the firms' shareholders (although some shareholders may also be customers), a mutual fund has no customers other than the owners who have invested their savings in shares of the fund. You can only benefit from the services of a mutual fund if you become a shareholder of the fund.

Avoid purchasing mutual fund shares just prior to an end-of-year capital gains distribution. A distribution will cause you to incur a tax liability even though you have gained no additional value.

The Structure of a Mutual Fund

A special corporate structure allows a mutual fund to continuously stand ready to sell shares of ownership, either to new investors or to existing shareholders, and to redeem outstanding shares of ownership. Thus, investors can generally purchase additional shares of a mutual fund at the same time that existing shareholders can "cash out," or have their shares redeemed. A few mutual funds have stopped selling shares to new investors, but these "closed" funds are a rarity.

A typical corporation (other than a mutual fund) infrequently issues new shares of its own stock. A company may issue shares of stock in an initial public offering and then not sell additional shares for many years. Established corporations that retain much of their profits for reinvestment in new assets may not sell additional shares for decades. Likewise, most corporations repurchase their shares only occasionally or not at all, causing shareholders who wish to sell their shares to seek other investors who are interested in buying them. A shareholder who wishes to sell shares of stock must normally use the services of a brokerage firm that has access to other investors through various securities markets.

A mutual fund's ability to sell additional shares of its own stock and to redeem its outstanding shares on demand stems both from the fund's corporate structure and from the nature of the assets it holds. Many stock and bond issues are actively traded, which allows mutual fund portfolio managers to invest additional shareholder contributions and to sell stocks and bonds from the fund's portfolio. Additional stocks and bonds are acquired when a mutual fund issues more shares than it redeems. Securities have to be sold from a mutual fund's portfolio when the fund is required to redeem more of its own shares than it sells. So long as there is an active market in the securities a mutual fund owns, the fund managers should not have great difficulty in increasing or decreasing the size of the fund's portfolio.

The typical manufacturing or service company owns many assets that would be difficult to sell on short notice. These companies could not operate effectively if the managers knew they might be required to sell portions of the assets whenever their shareholders decided to redeem shares. Likewise, most companies (other than mutual funds) are unable to acquire additional assets whenever investors decide they would like to purchase more shares of stock.

Mutual Fund Decision Making

A mutual fund is governed by directors who are elected by the fund's stockholders. The directors are responsible for hiring managers who oversee day-to-day operations of the fund. The directors are also responsible for making certain that the managers pursue the fund's stated investment objectives. The managers are normally paid a percentage of the amount of assets they manage. Successful managers (i.e., those who profiably invest shareholders' funds) will attract additional investors to buy shares in the fund, thereby increasing the size of the fund and the income of the managers. The more money the managers of a mutual fund are

> The most important rule of mutual fund investing is to select funds with investment goals that are similar to your own.

able to earn for the shareholders, the more money the managers will earn for themselves.

The directors of a mutual fund must select a *transfer agent* that will maintain shareholder records, issue new shares of stock, redeem outstanding shares of stock, and make payments to the fund's shareholders. The mutual fund must employ the services of a *custodian bank* or *trust company* to safeguard the fund's assets, make payments for securities purchases, and take charge of proceeds from the sale of securities. A single bank frequently serves both as custodian and transfer agent.

You hitch your financial wagon to the decisions of a mutual fund's portfolio managers when you invest in the fund's shares. The better the investment decisions that are made by a mutual fund's investment managers, the larger the return you will earn on your investment in the fund. Your shares will increase in value if the investment managers select stocks and bonds that rise in value. On the other hand, your shares will decline, or increase less than you expected, if a mutual fund's managers make poor investment decisions.

In summary, a mutual fund:

1. pools your funds with money contributed by hundreds or thousands of other investors who have similar investment goals;

2. provides for professional management of the fund's financial resources;

3. invests the shareholders' pooled monies in securities that are consistent with the fund's stated investment objectives;

4. pays dividends and capital gains distributions to the fund's shareholders from income that the fund earns.

Why Mutual Funds Are Popular Investments

There are several reasons to explain the tremendous increase in both the number of mutual funds and the amount of assets that these investment companies manage. Many individuals became acquainted with mutual fund investments in the mid- and late-1970s, when market interest rates were high relative to the interest rates that federal regulation allowed banks and savings and loan associations to pay on savings accounts. The comparatively low returns available on savings accounts caused individuals to move billions of dollars from depository financial institutions to specialized mutual funds that offered liquidity, safety, and relatively high yields. Investments in these narrowly focused funds helped open the gates to subsequent investments in equity (i.e., stock) and bond funds offered by many of the same fund sponsors.

Mutual funds that invest in stocks and bonds also benefited from increases in the market prices of these securities during the 1980s and 1990s. Strong markets for stocks and bonds attracted new investors who saw an opportunity to earn returns that were substantially higher than the returns being earned on their existing investments. While many individuals invested directly in stocks and bonds, others chose

Figure 2

MUTUAL FUND SHAREHOLDER ACCOUNTS

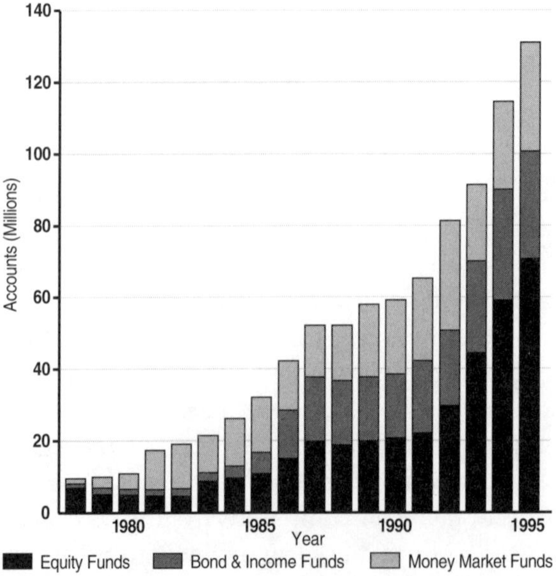

Source: Investment Company Institute, *Mutual Fund Fact Book*

to entrust their savings to the mutual funds that owned these investments. The high returns also encouraged individuals who already held mutual fund shares to invest additional money.

On an individual basis, mutual fund investments allow you to buy a single asset (i.e. shares of a mutual fund) and have the benefit of an investment that is spread among a large number of stocks and/or bonds. With only a relatively small amount of money, you achieve instant diversification by investing in a mutual fund. Mutual funds are also popular because many investors feel more comfortable having their money managed by professional money managers than investing on their own.

The Advantages of Professional Investment Management

Most people often find it difficult to make investment decisions regarding common stocks and bonds. If you are like most individual investors, your waking hours are consumed by short periods of relaxation sandwiched around your job; family responsibilities; and meetings of professional, charitable, and social organizations. You probably don't have enough free hours to study annual reports, read financial newsletters, and review brokerage house recommendations. Even professionals who work in the financial services industry often choose to have their personal funds managed by other professionals.

Without time to stay current on the investment scene, how can you possibly compete with other investors, especially professional money managers whose full-time job is to seek out undervalued stocks and bonds? Even when you are able to carve out some extra time to read financial reports, you may find it difficult to interpret all of the gobbledygook that fills most of them. You may be unsure about which securities to purchase, what price you should pay, and how long you should keep an investment. Should you adopt a buy-and-hold strategy in which you strive to make certain

> Attempt to avoid buying shares in a mutual fund that charges a 12b-1 fee, especially if you tend to hold your investments for long periods of time.

you purchase the "right" stocks or bonds and then hold these securities through thick and thin, or should you actively trade securities, moving your money from one security to another as you determine that some security prices are too low and others are too high? If you choose the latter course, how do you determine which securities to sell and when to sell them?

Rather than struggle with the many investment decisions that you should address when you purchase individual securities issues, you may be one of the many investors who decide to invest in shares of mutual funds and to trust the judgment of professional investment managers who are paid to supervise mutual fund portfolios. Mutual fund portfolio managers decide which securities to buy, how long to hold them, and which securities to replace them with when necessary. The managers decide when to adopt a conservative investment stance and when to invest more aggressively. The availability of professional investment managers means that, as an individual investor, you are required only to determine which managers to employ (i.e., what mutual fund to invest in) and when to make your investments. Subsequent chapters in this book discuss the wide variety of mutual funds that are available for purchase and how you should go about choosing among all these funds.

The Importance of Diversification

A great advantage of investing in mutual funds is the substantial diversification that you can achieve with a relatively small investment. When you purchase mutual fund shares, your investment is immediately spread among the many individual securities that are owned by the fund, a degree of diversification that would be impossible if you attempted to assemble a portfolio of your own. At any particular time a mutual fund typically owns a hundred or more different security issues; this provides substantial protection against major losses caused by declines in individual securities. For example, unfavorable news about a particular stock or a particular industry may have a negative effect on the market value of a mutual fund's portfolio, but the overall impact will be mitigated because the mutual fund's portfolio contains such a large number of securities, most of which remain unaffected by the news.

Most individual investors who purchase individual stock and bond issues are unable to achieve effective diversification unless they invest only small amounts of money in individual securities. For example, if you have $10,000 to invest and you wish to achieve even a minimal degree of diversification, you will need to limit your investment in each security to a small sum, causing you to incur relatively large commissions.

All mutual funds are not equally diversified. Many funds intentionally limit their diversification efforts by concentrating on investments in a particular industry or in companies that operate in a particular region of the United States or the world. Likewise, many mutual funds limit their investments to common stocks while other funds invest only in bonds or in both stocks and bonds. Specialized mutual funds offer much less diversification compared to mutual funds that invest in many different and diverse industries. Investing in the shares of specialized mutual funds results in a much greater likelihood that you will incur larger financial losses (or larger financial gains) compared to investors who choose nonspecialized funds.

The Ability to Shift Investments at Low Cost

Some mutual fund sponsors direct many different funds that have a wide range of investment objectives. For example, a single company may sponsor separate mutual funds that invest in money market securities, speculative stocks, high-grade bonds, tax-exempt securities, and junk bonds. Some sponsors oversee several different funds with similar investment objects. Sponsors of these *families of funds* generally permit shareholders of one fund to transfer their investment to one or more of the other funds for only a nominal fee. Suppose you have invested in the shares of a mutual fund specializing in growth stocks that is part of a family of funds, and you expect the stock market to decline during the next six months. You could redeem the shares of your stock fund and have the proceeds transferred to the shares of a money market fund or a short-term bond fund operated by the same sponsor.

Choosing to invest in individual securities (as opposed to mutual funds) can result in substantial brokerage fees, especially if you frequently trade investments. If you sell most or all of your shares of stock in order to move the money into intermediate-term bonds, you pay commissions to sell the stock, additional commissions to purchase the bonds, and yet another commission if you later decide to move the money back to the stock market. Mutual funds can facilitate these transfers, and the fees are often quite reasonable.

The Small Amount of Money Required for Investment

Nearly all mutual funds have established minimums for initial investments and for subsequent purchases of additional

Figure 3

SELECTED LIST OF LARGE MUTUAL FUND DISTRIBUTORS[1]

Alliance Fund Services
500 Plaza Drive
Secaucus, NJ 07094
800–221–5672

Colonial Investment Services
One Financial Center
Boston, MA 02111
800–225–2365

Dreyfus Service Corporation
144 Glenn Curtiss Boulevard
Uniondale, NY 11556
800–782–6620

Fidelity Distributors Corporation
82 Devonshire Street
Boston, MA 02109
800–544–6666

Flagship Financial
One First National Plaza, Suite 910
Dayton, OH 45402
800–227–4648

Franklin Distributors
777 Mariner's Island Boulevard, 6th Floor
San Mateo, CA 94404
800–632–2180

IDS Financial Services
IDS Tower 10
Minneapolis, MN 55440
800–328–8300

Kemper Financial Services
120 South LaSalle Street
Chicago, IL 60603
800–621–1048

Massachusetts Financial Services
PO Box 4657
Springfield, IL 62708
800–225–2606

John Nuveen & Company
333 West Wacker Drive
Chicago, IL 60606
800–621–7227

T. Rowe Price Associates
100 East Pratt Street
Baltimore, MD 21202
800–638–5660

Putnam Financial Services
PO Box 2701
Boston, MA 02208
800–225–1581

Scudder Fund Distributors
160 Federal Street
Boston, MA 02110
800–225–2470

Seligman Marketing
130 Liberty Street
New York, NY 10006
800–221–2450

USAA Investment Management
USAA Building
San Antonio, TX 78284
800–531–8181

Value Line Securities
711 Third Avenue, 4th Floor
New York, NY 10017
800–223–0818

Vanguard Group of Investment Companies
PO Box 2600
MS–136
Valley Forge, PA 19482
800–662–7447

[1]Most large broker–dealers distribute their own tax-exempt mutual funds. These distributors are excluded from this listing.

shares. Funds typically require an investment of from $250 to $2,500 (depending upon the fund) to establish an account, although some mutual funds have minimums of $10,000 and more. With some funds once you establish an account, you can buy additional shares with an investment as small as $50. Minimum investment requirements are established by each fund's sponsor.

Mutual Fund Services

Competition for investors has caused mutual funds to offer their shareholders a variety of useful services, often at no additional cost (although additional services that cost the sponsor money may ultimately reduce the returns earned by shareholders). The availability and details of each fund's services are spelled out in the free prospectus that you should obtain and study before you invest your money. The relative value of each service depends upon your investment needs. You may find you have little need for a specific service that many other investors consider nearly indispensable. Some of the more popular services offered by mutual funds include the following.

Check-writing privileges is a service made available by most money market funds and by many bond funds. Funds that offer check writing generally establish a minimum amount (typically $500 or $1,000) for which a check can be written, and a few funds charge a nominal fee for each check you write. Some funds set a limit on the number of checks you are permitted to write each month. Check writing is the ultimate method for redeeming your shares in a mutual fund. Rather than request that the fund send you a

> Don't make the mistake of choosing a tax-exempt money market or bond fund unless you are certain your marginal tax rate is at a high enough level for you to benefit from the tax exemption.

check in the mail or ask that money be wired to your bank account, you merely write a check to pay for a good or service you purchase or to deposit funds in your bank account. The check is processed through the federal reserve's check-clearing system and presented for payment to your mutual fund's transfer agent, which will redeem the appropriate number of shares required to cover the check. Your investment at the mutual fund continues to earn interest until the check is presented for payment.

Automatic investing allows you to arrange for a mutual fund distributor to regularly transfer money from your bank account in order to buy shares in the fund. Some mutual fund distributors permit you to acquire shares through automatic payroll deductions from your paycheck. Automatic investing is a good way to implement a dollar-cost averaging system like that discussed in Chapter 7 and illustrated in Figure 21.

Reinvestment of dividends and capital gains distributions is an option made available by most mutual funds. Choosing to reinvest your dividends and capital gains distributions in additional shares of the fund is similar to reinvesting interest from a savings account; both actions will cause the value of your account to grow more rapidly. Reinvestment is practical only when you do not require current investment income to meet living expenses. Many mutual fund investors choose to receive dividends and reinvest capital gains distributions.

Wire transfers are permitted by many mutual funds. A wire transfer allows you to rapidly transfer money to or from a mutual fund. For example, you can request that shares be sold and the proceeds wired to your bank account or brokerage account so that you have instant access to the funds. You will be required to request wire transfer privileges before you are able to access this service, and there may be a nominal charge for each wire transfer you initiate.

Exchanges, also called *switching*, is a handy method for moving all or a portion of your money out of one mutual fund and into the shares of another mutual fund operated by the same company. Switching between funds was mentioned briefly in the previous discussion of families of funds. Suppose you have placed all your money in a mutual fund that invests in long-term corporate bonds but have now decided that you would like to move a portion of your money into growth stocks. If you have invested with a mutual fund sponsor that operates several other funds, you may be able to switch your investment from the bond fund to a growth stock fund with no more than a telephone call and at only a small fee. Mutual fund sponsors that offer exchange privileges generally require transfers of a minimum size and sometimes establish restrictions on the number of exchanges you can make during a given period of time.

Retirement accounts are offered by most mutual funds. Mutual funds have become one of the major players in the market for Individual Retirement Accounts (IRAs), self-employed retirement plans (Keogh plans), corporate retirement plans (401(k) plans), and rollovers from existing IRAs or pension plans. Mutual funds have varying charges for establishing and servicing different types of retirement plans.

Regulation of Mutual Funds

Mutual funds are subject to substantial regulation at several levels. The initial regulation affecting investment companies was passed during the 1930s and was occasioned by excesses in the industry prior to the Great Crash of 1929. Mutual fund regulation is primarily designed to make certain that the funds operate in a responsible manner and that investors have the opportunity to learn about the fees, investment policies, and past performance of a particular mutual fund. Neither federal nor state regulation ensures that a mutual fund's advisers will render good investment advice or that your investment in a fund's shares will prove profitable.

At the federal level the Securities Act of 1933, also called the "Truth in Securities Act," requires all issuers of new securities and some secondary offerings, including mutual funds, to file with the federal government a registration statement that provides extensive details about the company. The act also requires that a mutual fund provide investors with a current prospectus describing the fund's policies and investment objectives. The primary purpose of this act is to make certain that companies issuing securities provide full disclosure of relevant information so that investors have the opportunity to make informed investment decisions.

The following year Congress passed the Securities Exchange Act of 1934, which established the Securities and Exchange Commission (SEC) and vested the organization with a variety of enforcement powers. The 1934 act extended disclosure requirements to securities that are traded in the secondary markets (e.g., the over-the-counter market and organized exchanges such as the New York Stock Exchange). Mutual fund distributors are subject to regulation by the National Association of Securities Dealers (NASD) and the Securities and Exchange Commission.

The Investment Company Act of 1940 is one of the major pieces of legislation that provides for the federal regulation of mutual funds. The 1940 act requires mutual funds to (1) provide investors with accurate information, (2) guarantee that shareholders will have a say in certain matters affecting the funds, (3) use approved accounting methods, (4) maintain adequate liquidity, (5) operate in the interest of shareholders, and (6) refrain from levying excessive fees and charges. Separate legislation produced the Investment Advisors Act of 1940, which regulates the activities of mutual fund advisers.

The Investment Company Amendments Act of 1970 imposes a fiduciary standard on the managers, officers, and directors of an investment company. The act also facilitates a shareholder protest of sales charges and other expenses.

Mutual funds are also subject to regulation by the states in which they are organized and the states in which shares are distributed to investors. Individuals who distribute mutual fund shares are subject to federal and state regulation.

Income and Taxation

The bottom line to any investment is the after-tax return you earn. The income you earn from an investment must be considered in light of the taxes you will be required to pay on the income. Mutual funds can potentially produce three types of income for shareholders. In most instances this income is taxable to the shareholders but not to the mutual funds.

Sources of Income for Mutual Fund Shareholders

There are three possible sources of income for an investor who owns shares in a mutual fund:

1. Dividends that the mutual fund pays from the dividend and interest income earned on its own investments. For example, a mutual fund will receive dividends from stocks that it owns and interest from bonds that it owns. Virtually all of this dividend and interest income is passed through to the mutual fund's shareholders as dividend payments. Dividends may be paid monthly or quarterly depending on the fund.
2. Capital gains distributions paid to stockholders when securities owned by the mutual fund are sold at a gain. For example, if a mutual fund purchases 50,000 shares of Coca-Cola common stock for $38 per share and subsequently sells the stock for $48 per share, the fund earns a capital gain of $500,000 (50,000 shares at a gain of $10 per share) that can be distributed to the fund's shareholders. Capital gains distributions are generally made once each year.
3. Increases in the value of the mutual fund's shares that result from increases in the values of securities the fund owns. If the mutual fund invests in securities that subsequently increase in value, the value of the mutual fund's shares will also increase. In the previous example, if the fund's managers decided to retain the Coca-Cola shares,

> Make a mutual fund's fee structure one of the most important considerations in your choice of a mutual fund.

the mutual fund's own shares would have greater value because the fund's portfolio would have a greater market value.

Taxation of Mutual Fund Income

A mutual fund that meets Internal Revenue Service requirements to qualify as a regulated investment company is not required to pay taxes on the dividends, interest, and capital gains the fund earns. Regulated investment companies are nothing but conduits that pass income along to their shareholders who are required to pay taxes on the income at rates based on their personal income. To qualify as a regulated investment company, a mutual fund must comply with certain regulations regarding asset diversification and must distribute at least 90 percent of its taxable income to shareholders.

In general, ordinary income earned by a mutual fund is taxed as ordinary income to the shareholders while capital gains earned by a fund are taxed as capital gains to the shareholders. For example, if you pay federal income taxes at a rate of 28 percent, you will pay taxes at a rate of 28 percent on dividend distributions received from a mutual fund. Mutual fund distributions of income not normally taxable to individuals (e.g., interest on municipal bonds) remain nontaxable when they are received by shareholders. If you have chosen to have your distributions automatically reinvested in additional shares of stock, you must pay taxes on these distributions just as if you had received them.

A gain in the market value of a mutual fund's shares is not taxable until the shares are sold. The difference between the price paid to purchase the shares and the price received from the sale of the shares determines the amount of income that is subject to taxation. So long as you continue to hold mutual fund shares, you will not be taxed on any gains or losses in the value of your shares.

At the end of each year, mutual funds are required to send each stockholder a form that lists the types and amounts of distributions sent to the stockholder during the year. Information on distributions to individual shareholders is also forwarded to the Internal Revenue Service, which will use these data to check the accuracy of your tax return.

Determining the Cost Basis of the Shares You Sell

When you eventually sell shares of a mutual fund, you will need to compute the gain or loss that will be reported to the Internal Revenue Service on Schedule D of your federal tax return. Calculating a gain or loss requires that you determine the cost, or *basis*, of the shares you sold. The amount of the gain or loss is determined by subtracting the cost from the price you receive when the shares are sold. The problem you will sometimes encounter is determining which shares of a single fund you sold.

The gain or loss is easy to calculate when all of your shares have been purchased at the same price. Suppose you purchase 1,000 shares at a price of $15.20 and sell half these shares at a price of $20.00. You decide to retain the other 500 shares. Your gain is $4.80 per share ($20.00 less your cost of $15.20) times the 500 shares you sold, or $2,400. This is the amount that will be taxed. The $15.20

Figure 4

DETERMINING GAINS FROM THE SALE OF MUTUAL FUND SHARES

Suppose you purchase shares in the Beuther Growth Fund over a period of several years. The record of your purchases is as follows:

Date Purchased	Amount Invested	Price	Shares Bought	Shares Owned
3/07/92	$ 5,000.00	$15.00	333.333	333.333
6/15/92	3,000.00	14.50	206.897	540.230
8/20/92	2,500.00	15.10	165.563	705.793
11/10/92	2,800.00	15.30	183.007	888.800
12/15/92*	844.36	16.25	51.961	940.761
2/09/93	2,000.00	16.12	124.069	1,064.830
6/28/93	2,500.00	15.75	158.730	1,223.560
7/10/93	600.00	16.50	36.364	1,259.924
10/12/93	3,000.00	16.75	179.104	1,439.028

* reinvestment of 95 cents per share distribution

The total amount invested is $22,244.36
The average cost per share is $15.45 ($22,244.36/1,439.028 shares)

A. Suppose on 12/1/93 you sell all of your shares at the current price of $17.00 per share. Your total gain equals the gain per share ($17.00 minus $15.45, or $1.55) times the number of shares you sell (1,439.028), or $2,230.49. Gains from the sale of shares that have been held over one year (888.800 shares x $1.55, or $1,377.64) qualify as long-term. The remaining portion of the gain is short-term.

Figure 4 (continued)

An alternative is to compute the average cost for shares held over a year and use this cost to determine your long-term gain, and to compute the average cost for shares held a year or less and use this cost to determine your short-term gain.

B. Suppose on 12/1/93 you sell 800 shares at the current price of $17.00 per share. The three methods for determining your cost basis produce the following gains that can be used to calculate your taxes.

1. Average price—The total gain equals the sale price minus the average cost ($17.00 - $15.45, or $1.55) times the number of shares sold (800), or $1,240.00.
2. First bought, first sold—Calculate the gain for each group of shares to a total of 800 shares, beginning with the first shares purchased. Using the information provided in the purchase record, you have a gain of $2.00 per share ($17.00 - $15.00) on the first 333.333 shares, $2.50 per share ($17.00 - $14.50) on the next 206.897 shares, $1.90 ($17.00 - $15.10) on the next 165.563 shares, and $1.70 ($17.00 - $15.30) on 94.207 of the 183.007 shares purchased on 11/10/92. The total gain of $1,658.63 is classified as long-term because all of the shares sold have been held over a year.
3. Selected shares—If you intend to minimize the gain reported to tax authorities, you should request that the mutual fund sell shares that have the highest cost. Request the fund to sell 179.104 shares bought at $16.75, 36.364 shares bought at $16.50, 51.961 shares purchased for $16.25, 124.069 shares bought at $16.12, 158.730 shares purchased at $15.75, 183.007 shares bought for $15.30 each, and 66.765 of the 165.563 shares bought at $15.10. The total gain using this approach is $852.49.

If you believe that tax rates are going to increase in the near future, you may wish to direct the fund to sell shares with the lowest cost, not the highest cost. Selling shares acquired at the lowest cost would increase your current taxable gain but would decrease the taxable gain in some future year when you sell the remainder of the shares.

cost basis of the remaining shares will be used when these shares are sold at some later date.

If you sell all the shares you have accumulated at many different prices, as would be the case if you have reinvested dividend and capital gains distributions, the calculation of gains or losses is somewhat more complicated because you have many different cost bases. Still, there will be a record of the prices you have paid, so you shouldn't have great difficulty in calculating gains or losses. Suppose you purchased a hundred shares of a mutual fund at a price of $14.00 per share and acquired an additional four shares at $14.50 per share and another five shares at $15.00 per share. If you sell all the shares at a price of $17.00, your total gain will be $300 + $10 + $10, or $320. Another method of arriving at the same gain is to calculate the average price you paid for the shares and then subtract this price from the price at which your shares have been sold. You then multiply the difference times the number of shares you sold.

When you sell only a portion of the shares you have acquired at several different prices, you are presented with a real challenge in determining the gains or losses. Suppose you originally purchased 600 shares at a price of $15.20, but you purchased an additional 400 shares at varying prices over the course of many years. Now, when you sell 500 shares of your mutual fund, which shares are you selling, and what basis do you use? Are you selling 500 of the original shares, or are you selling 100 of the original shares and 400 shares acquired through reinvestment? Determining which shares you sold may seem a pointless exercise, but the truth is you must arrive at a cost basis for the shares you sell to calculate your income tax liability.

Actually, there are several acceptable methods for determining the cost basis of mutual fund shares that you sell. These are:

1. *First acquired, first sold*—Unless otherwise indicated, the Internal Revenue Service assumes that the first shares acquired are the first shares sold. This method assumes that you have sold 500 of your original shares.
2. *Average cost*—Divide the total amount you have invested in all the shares you currently own by the number of shares of the mutual fund you currently own to determine the average cost of the shares. Subtract the average cost from the price at which shares are sold to determine your gain or loss per share.
3. *Specific shares*—Instruct the mutual fund to sell shares that you acquired on specific dates and use the cost of these shares to determine the size of your gain or loss. You can minimize your reported gain and your immediate tax liability if you direct the fund to sell shares that have the highest cost bases. If you reduce your immediate tax liability, you are likely to increase your future tax liability. This may or may not be a good idea.

CHAPTER 2

The Operation and Valuation of a Mutual Fund

The value of a mutual fund's shares is determined by the total value of the fund's securities portfolio (its only assets) and the number of outstanding shares of the mutual fund's stock. The share value determines the price shareholders will receive for redeemed shares and the price investors will pay for new shares. The size of a mutual fund's portfolio expands and contracts as investors purchase and redeem the fund's shares. The redemption of outstanding shares and sale of new shares have little effect on shareholders who continue to hold their shares.

Chapter 1 explained that mutual funds are structured in an unusual fashion compared to other corporations. A mutual fund continuously offers new shares of stock for sale at the same time that the fund stands ready to redeem its outstanding shares. Mutual funds have this flexibility because of the great liquidity of the assets they hold. The continuous and active market in most stock and bond issues permits a mutual fund's managers to readily invest new money and to sell securities from the fund's portfolio.

Depending upon whether investors are, on balance, buying new shares or redeeming outstanding shares of a particular mutual fund, the total value of the fund's portfolio (but not necessarily per-share value) will expand or contract. Management that is adept at selecting securities that appreciate in value will attract new investors to the fund at the same time that current shareholders are likely to be buying more shares than they are redeeming. A mutual fund that issues many additional shares of its stock will swell in size and require the fund's portfolio managers to invest substantial amounts of new money. Investment managers who do a poor job of selecting securities are likely to cause investor redemptions that exceed the sale of new shares, thereby causing a reduction in the fund's size. The linkage is clear: In the mutual fund business, the good get bigger and the bad get smaller. Several years of superior investment performance can cause a mutual fund to grow to many times its previous size.

The best way to explain the organization and operation of a mutual fund is to take a step-by-step journey that begins at the time a fund is conceived and carries through the time when investment managers begin making changes to the composition of the portfolio.

> Most individual investors are best served by utilizing a buy-and-hold strategy unless their investment goals change.

Establishing the Grits Fund

Suppose you and a group of your semiwealthy associates decide to pool your investment capital and establish an investment company you call the Grits Fund. Members of the group have grown weary of managing their investments on an individual basis. You and your associates have spent many hours discussing the high brokerage commissions you pay, the generally poor investment advice you receive, and the losses you have suffered on your investments. You have finally concluded that a collective effort should produce improved investment results.

Investing as a group should produce savings on brokerage commissions because of the smaller proportional fees charged by brokerage firms for stock transactions that involve greater amounts of money. More importantly, you expect improved investment performance because your group is planning to enlist the services of an experienced money manager who will select and manage a portfolio of securities for your benefit. You feel that having investment decisions made by a full-time professional money manager will produce superior results compared to the returns that each member of the investment group has been able to accomplish individually.

Investors in the Grits Fund will be allocated ownership of the fund on the basis of their proportional contribution. Initially, there will be twenty owners, including yourself, who will each contribute a minimum of $10,000. The members have decided to issue the initial shares of ownership at a price of $10, although subsequent sales will occur at prices determined by the value of the company's portfolio of investments and the number of outstanding shares. The Grits Fund will accept investments from new owners, and it will permit existing shareholders to purchase additional shares of stock. Likewise, shareholders may redeem, at any time, all or any portion of their shares. The method by which the fund's share price is established and the fund's shares are redeemed is addressed later in this chapter.

Establishing the Fund's Investment Objective

It is crucial that your personal investment objectives are consistent with the objectives of the other members of your group and with the investment philosophy of the fund you will be joining. If most members of your group desire to have the fund invest in speculative stocks and pursue high returns and you don't have the financial resources or the stomach for the potentially large losses that can result from this type of investing, you should look for a different investment. You should investigate a number of things prior to investing in a mutual fund, but none is more important than the fund's investment objective.

Suppose that you and the other members of your investment group are unanimous in your desire to pursue a goal of capital growth with moderate risk. Current income is determined to be a secondary objective. The fund will achieve capital growth by investing in the stocks of companies that are market leaders and are expected to have rising earnings and increasing stock prices. The members decide to concentrate the fund's investments in the stocks of companies that operate primarily in the Southeast (hence, the fund name). The stated objectives and means of achieving these objectives will restrict the flexibility of the Grits Fund's investment managers, who will be forced to choose among stocks that offer only modest current dividend income. The manager will also be unable to invest large amounts of the fund's money in promising companies outside the Southeast. The members of your group will inform the investment manager to keep brokerage commissions low by minimizing portfolio turnover.

Putting Together the Grits Fund

Suppose that the twenty investors in your group contribute total investment capital of $400,000. Although you and some of the other investors have each decided to contribute only $10,000, several individuals will invest up to $40,000 each. The total combined investment will require that the fund initially issue 40,000 shares of stock valued at $10 each. The fund could equally well have issued 20,000 shares at a price of $20 each or 10,000 shares at a price of $40 each. You and the other investors choose an initial price of $10 because $10 seems to be a price that appeals to investors who purchase investment company shares.

Money contributed by the owners will be placed initially in highly liquid investments such as Treasury bills or a money market fund while the investment manager deter-

> Beware of bond funds that have been paying unusually high current returns to their shareholders. High current returns are often the result of owning risky investments.

mines which stocks to include in the fund's portfolio. Balances in the short-term investments will gradually decline as money is withdrawn to invest in growth stocks; however, the fund will need to maintain some short-term balances to pay its operating expenses (light bills, rent, telephone bills), to pay the investment manager's salary, and to pay for shares that are presented for redemption.

The investment manager's view of the stock market is another factor that will influence the proportion of the fund's assets that is maintained in short-term investments. A fund manager who feels the stock market is generally overvalued and poised for a decline is likely to maintain a substantial portion of the fund's assets in Treasury bills. When conditions have changed sufficiently to convince the manager that stocks have bottomed out and will be headed upward, the manager will sell the Treasury bills and use the proceeds to add growth stocks to the fund's portfolio. A fund manager who feels the outlook for the stock market is favorable is likely to be fully invested in anticipation of increasing stock prices. A major part of a portfolio manager's job is determining the most favorable times to invest.

The Initial Portfolio

Suppose the investment manager decides to make the Grits Fund easier to manage (and easier for the author to explain) by limiting the fund's portfolio at any given time to no more than ten stocks. The limited portfolio of the Grits Fund compares to 50 to 100, or even more stocks that are owned by the typical mutual fund. Figure 5 displays the contents and value of the Grits Fund's initial portfolio.

Figure 5 indicates that of $400,000 initially contributed

Figure 5

INITIAL PORTFOLIO OF THE GRITS FUND

Stock	Div.	Shares	Price	Value
Coca-Cola	$ .56	1,000	$39¼	$ 39,250
Digital Equipment	—	1,300	34	44,200
Disney	.21	1,200	40¼	48,300
Flowers Industries	.73	1,000	20	20,000
Georgia Pacific	1.60	800	57⅝	46,100
Home Depot	.12	600	59	35,400
NationsBank	1.60	400	46⅞	18,750
Philip Morris	2.60	700	78⅛	54,687
Shoneys	—	1,300	22¾	29,575
Winn Dixie	1.32	500	68⅜	34,187
Total Stock Portfolio Value				$370,449
Short-Term Investments				$27,649
Total Fund Value				$398,098
Shares Outstanding				40,000
Net Asset Value				$9.95

by investors, $370,449 has been invested in common stock and $27,649 remains in short-term investments such as Treasury bills or other money market securities. The remainder of the initial shareholder contributions ($1,902) has been consumed by brokerage commissions that average .5 percent of the principal amount invested. For example, $39,250 that was invested in Coca-Cola stock caused the fund to pay a brokerage commission of $196. The ten transactions caused the Grits Fund to incur brokerage commissions of $1,952, money that has been paid from the fund's initial $400,000 and is no longer available for investing.

Mutual fund shares are valued by calculating the *net asset value (NAV)*, the total market value of the fund's assets divided by the number of the fund's outstanding shares. Figure 5 shows that the NAV of the Grits Fund is $398,098 divided by 40,000 shares, or $9.95. Net asset value establishes the price at which new shares will be sold to investors (unless a sales charge is added) and the price at which outstanding shares will be redeemed. A particular fund's NAV constantly changes as the securities held in the fund's portfolio vary in price. An increase in the market prices of the securities held in the fund's portfolio causes a corresponding increase in the net asset value of the fund's shares. Conversely, a decline in the prices of securities owned by the fund causes the fund's net asset value to fall.

In the unlikely event that the Grits Fund maintains exactly the same portfolio during the entire first year of its operation, $6,014 in dividends will be received from the ten securities that are owned (actually, only eight stocks pay dividends). Assuming all the dividends are passed through to the fund's stockholders, each share of outstanding stock will earn a dividend of 15 cents ($6,014/40,000 shares). Thus, the 1,000 shares of the fund's stock that you purchased for the minimum initial investment of $10,000 will earn $150 of dividends during the first year you hold the stock. The current return on your initial investment is $150 in annual dividends divided by $10,000, or 1.5 percent. This is a modest current return, but you must take into consideration the fact that the fund's goal is capital growth, not current income.

Figure 6

VALUATION OF THE GRITS FUND AFTER ONE YEAR

Stock	Div.	Shares	Price	Value
Coca-Cola	$ .56	1,000	$45½	$ 45,500
Digital Equipment	—	1,300	36⅛	46,962
Disney	.21	1,200	40½	48,600
Flowers Industries	.73	1,000	25⅛	25,125
Georgia Pacific	1.60	800	56½	45,200
Home Depot	.12	600	62⅜	37,425
NationsBank	1.60	400	46	18,400
Philip Morris	2.60	700	84½	59,150
Shoneys	—	1,300	20¾	26,975
Winn Dixie	1.32	500	70⅞	35,437
Total Stock Portfolio Value				$388,774
Short-Term Investments				$ 28,649
Total Fund Value				$417,423
Shares Outstanding				40,000
Net Asset Value				$10.44

How Changes in Stock Prices Affect Net Asset Value

Suppose that twelve months pass and the composition of the Grits Fund portfolio remains unchanged. Although the fund continues to hold the same securities, the market values of each of the stocks have changed. The new stock prices and portfolio value are illustrated in Figure 6.

The $19,325 increase in the value of the fund's securities results in $417,423 of total fund assets and a net asset value

> Avoid aggressive growth funds unless you are willing to accept the large variations in value that these shares exhibit.

of $417,423/40,000 shares, or $10.44. You now own 1,000 shares worth $10.44 each, for a total value of $10,440. You have earned a total return of $150 (15 cents per share dividends paid to you by the fund) plus $440 in the appreciation of your shares ($10,440 current value less your $10,000 original investment), or 5.9 percent on your original $10,000 investment.

The fund's investment income and dividends to shareholders are actually likely to be lower than what is indicated here because there has been no accounting for expenses to operate and manage the fund. For example, the cost of employing the investment manager, paying the telephone bills, and so forth would ordinarily have to be paid from the fund's investment income, thereby reducing the dividends paid to the Grits Fund's shareholders. If the fund incurred expenses of $5,000, total dividends paid to shareholders would have been $1,014 rather than $6,014.

The Effect of Portfolio Changes on Net Asset Value

Portfolio turnover has no effect on net asset value except insomuch as (1) brokerage commissions paid by the fund to buy and sell securities reduce NAV, and (2) different securities can be expected to experience different price changes, thus influencing changes in the fund's NAV. If an investment manager replaces several securities with other securities that subsequently increase proportionately more in price than the securities that were sold, the fund's NAV and your investment in the fund will benefit with higher values.

To observe how swapping securities leaves the fund's net asset value unaffected, suppose at the end of the year the investment manager sells all the Coca-Cola stock and Shoneys stock held by the fund. The manager will probably transfer the $72,475 proceeds from the sale into short-term securities and subsequently reinvest in other stocks. Other than brokerage commissions that the fund must pay, neither the sale of the two stock positions nor the reinvestment of the proceeds in some other asset has any immediate effect on the total assets in the fund's portfolio and no effect on the fund's net asset value. Switching from one stock to another, or from a stock to a short-term investment, reallocates the portfolio's funds, but it does not increase or reduce the total value of the portfolio.

The Effect on NAV of Selling and Redeeming Shares of the Fund's Stock

Your investment in a mutual fund remains unaffected when the fund sells additional shares of stock or redeems a portion of the fund's outstanding shares so long as the net asset value is used to price the shares that are sold or redeemed. Because changes in outstanding shares will not affect your financial position, you generally have no cause for concern when new investors purchase additional shares of the fund or when current stockholders exit the fund by cashing in their shares.

Selling Additional Shares of the Fund's Stock

As mentioned previously, the managers of a mutual fund are compensated based on the amount of assets they supervise. Their compensation is generally established as a percentage of the assets in the fund's portfolio, although the percentage may decline somewhat as the total assets surpass specified levels. The assets in a portfolio increase as individual securities held by the fund increase in price and as investors purchase additional shares in the fund. Thus, it is to the investment managers' financial advantage to produce above-average investment performance that will bring new investors into the fund at the same time that it will increase the value of the fund's assets.

Issuing new shares of the Grits Fund to existing or outside investors will not change the value of your own shares because it will not change the fund's net asset value. Suppose we consider an instance in which a new investor purchases 1,000 shares of the fund's stock. The fund issues 1,000 additional shares, causing the fund's total outstanding shares to increase from 40,000 to 41,000. The new investor is required to pay $10,440, or $10.44 per share, the current net asset value, for each share purchased. Following the issue of the new shares, the fund owns a portfolio valued at $417,423 plus the additional $10,440, or $427,863. The net asset value remains at $427,863 divided by 11,000 shares, or $10.44.

> Mutual funds are excellent vehicles for investing overseas where information is often scarce and costs of acquiring individual investments tend to be high.

The investment manager must find a use for the new money invested in the fund, which means that more shares of stock must be added to the fund's portfolio. The new money may be placed temporarily in short-term investments while various stock investments are evaluated, or the money may be invested immediately in shares of stock. The manager will not normally want a large portion of the fund's portfolio in short-term assets that earn relatively low returns, especially given the fund's investment objective of capital growth.

Redeeming the Fund's Outstanding Shares

Redemptions of outstanding shares have the opposite effect on the fund's portfolio from sales of additional shares. A redemption requires that the investment manager pay money to the selling stockholder in return for retiring the shares presented for redemption. If a relatively small number of shares are redeemed, short-term investments are tapped to provide the necessary money. Otherwise, the investment manager must sell shares from the fund's stock portfolio to raise the required amount of money.

Suppose a stockholder decides to sell 2,000 shares back to the Grits Fund at the end of the first year of operation. The mutual fund's investment manager must come up with $20,880 (2,000 shares at a NAV of $10.44), which is somewhat less than the $28,649 the fund has available in short-term investments. The investment manager could redeem the 2,000 shares without selling any stock from the fund's portfolio. On the other hand, the manager may feel that the fund should always maintain liquidity by holding at least $20,000 in short-term assets.

Figure 7

EFFECT OF SHAREHOLDER REDEMPTION

	Year-End Values	After Stock Sale	After Redemption
Short-Term Investments	$ 28,649	$ 47,049	$ 26,169
Stock Portfolio	$388,774	$370,374	$370,374
Total Fund Assets	$417,423	$417,423	$396,543
Shares Outstanding	40,000	40,000	38,000
Net Asset Value	$10.44	$10.44	$10.44

To meet the self-established liquidity requirement, the investment manager decides to sell the fund's entire 400-share position in NationsBank common stock, which nets $18,400 for the fund. When $18,400 in proceeds from the stock sale are added to existing short-term assets of $28,649, total short-term investments climb to $47,049. To this point there is no change in the net asset value of the Grits Fund because total fund assets and shares outstanding each remain unchanged. The fund manager has merely transferred $18,400 from common stocks to short-term investments.

While portfolio turnover does not affect either fund assets or outstanding shares of the fund, selling or redeeming shares of the fund changes both these variables. When the fund pays out $20,880 for 2,000 shares of its own stock, total fund assets will decline by $20,880, to $396,543, while outstanding shares of the fund's stock will drop by 2,000, to 38,000. Even though the fund's total assets and shares outstanding are each reduced by the redemption, the net asset value of the fund remains at $10.44 because the reduction in assets is exactly offset by a proportional reduction in outstanding shares. Neither the sale of additional shares nor the redemption of outstanding shares affects the net asset value of a mutual fund's shares. A summary of the effects of the transactions just discussed is illustrated in Figure 7.

Thus, portfolio turnover, share redemptions, and the sale of additional shares do not have a discernible effect on the Grits Fund's net asset value, the measure of the fund's value that is most important to you. New investors can buy into the fund and current investors can liquidate their shares without disturbing your own investment in the fund. Portfolio turnover will have some effect because the fund pays brokerage commissions when stocks are bought and sold. Also, redemptions and sales of new shares sometimes have an effect on the way a fund is managed. As funds grow larger, their portfolio managers lose flexibility in the investments they can choose.

The Effect of Dividends and Capital Gains Distributions

Sales and redemptions of the fund's shares do not affect your mutual fund investment because they do not affect the fund's assets on a per-share basis. On the other hand, distri-

> Don't buy shares in a growth fund or an aggressive growth fund based only on the most recent year's investment performance. Short-term performance is a poor indicator of future near-term performance.

butions by a mutual fund do affect your investment. Both dividend payments and capital gain distributions reduce a mutual fund's net asset value.

Dividend Payments

A dividend payment to a company's stockholders reduces the price of the firm's stock by the amount of the dividend payment. For example, a 75-cent dividend to stockholders causes the price of the firm's common stock to fall by an equal amount, three-quarters of a point. The stock price is reduced because the dividend payment leaves the company with a smaller amount of assets on which to earn income in subsequent periods. Your overall wealth as a stockholder of the firm is unaffected by a dividend payment because the reduction in the value of your stock is offset by the dividend you receive.

If the wealth of individual stockholders is not affected by dividend payments, the wealth of a mutual fund, which is itself a stockholder, is also unaffected by dividend payments on the stocks that it holds in its portfolio, at least initially. When a stock owned by a mutual fund pays a dividend, the mutual fund's stock portfolio declines in value (because the stock on which the dividend is paid declines in market price) at the same time that the fund's short-term investments are supplemented by the dividend received. Thus, the fund's net asset value and your investment in the fund are unaffected by dividend payments to the mutual fund.

So how is your investment in a mutual fund affected when the mutual fund pays a dividend to its own stockholders? It was mentioned earlier that mutual funds typically pass through to their own stockholders all, or nearly all, of the dividends and interest they receive. The effect of a mutual fund's dividend payment is identical to the effect of a dividend payment on an individual stock that you own. That is, the value of your investment in the fund will decline by the amount of the dividend you receive. Suppose you own 200 shares in a mutual fund that has a net asset value of $14.50 per share. If the fund pays a dividend of 75 cents per share, the fund's net asset value will decline by 75 cents, to $13.75 per share. The total value of your shares declines by $150 (75 cents times 200 shares), a sum that is identical to the dividend income you receive.

Capital Gains Distributions

Capital gains have no effect on a mutual fund's value until the gains are distributed to shareholders. The distribution of gains has the same effect as the payment of dividends. That is, a capital gain distribution reduces the assets of the fund and the net asset value of the fund's shares. The NAV reduction is equal to the amount of the gain distributed to shareholders. If a mutual fund pays a $1.20 per share capital gain distribution, the fund's total assets will decline by $1.20 times the number of outstanding shares, and the net asset value will decline by $1.20 per share. The value of your investment in the fund is reduced by an amount equal to the cash distribution you receive. Thus, you are no better off nor any worse off after the capital gains distribution than you were before the distribution. Sort of.

Taxation of Distributions

The problem with dividends and capital gains distributions

is that you will be taxed on the money you receive (unless you receive dividends from a fund that invests in tax-exempt securities). Thus, a distribution causes you to incur a tax liability that reduces the value of your total holdings because the amount of additional cash you have left after taxes will be less than the declines in the value of your mutual fund shares. Suppose you buy shares of a mutual fund just prior to a major capital gains distribution. You receive the distribution at the same time that the net asset value of your shares declines by an offsetting amount. However, you now have a tax liability on the distribution you received that will cause a reduction in your overall wealth.

You would be in a better financial position if the mutual fund reinvested the dividends it received rather than passing them along to you. However, special tax exemptions are accorded only to mutual funds that distribute the dividends they receive to their shareholders.

CHAPTER 3

Equity Funds

Equity funds—mutual funds that invest in common stocks—have been, until recent years, the clear choice of individual investors who trusted their money to the care of investment companies. Although equity funds (also called *stock funds* and *common stock funds*) are often subject to large changes in value, investors are attracted to the large potential returns they can earn from owning common stocks. The value of an equity fund is equal to the combined values of the individual stocks that the fund owns. There are many different categories of stock funds that provide different investment returns and subject mutual fund shareholders to different risks. You should select an equity fund that has an investment goal that is compatible with your own financial needs.

Figure 8

NUMBER OF MUTUAL FUNDS, BY TYPE

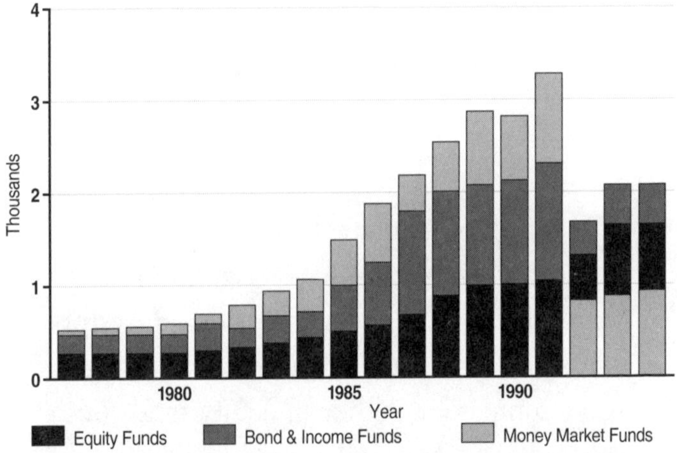

Source: Investment Company Institute, *Mutual Fund Fact Book*

When you read an article or overhear a discussion concerning mutual funds, your thoughts are likely to turn to common stocks even though mutual funds that invest in equities now comprise only a little over a third of all investment companies (see Figure 8). The connection between mutual funds and common stocks is to some extent caused by the large price changes of equity fund shares and the resulting fanfare these funds receive in the media. Just as bettors at a horse track talk mostly about the long shots they hit, mutual fund investors are more prone to discuss the 20 to 30 percent returns they earn from common stock funds than the 8 percent returns from bond funds or the 5 percent earned from money market funds. Although individuals are less likely to talk about major losses of any kind, the financial media have never been shy about reporting on equity funds that sustain large losses in value. Stock funds are where the action is!

Historically, equity funds have been the investment of choice among investors. It was not until the mid-1980s that equity funds were surpassed by bond and income funds in both the number of funds and the amount of assets under management. Many investors who choose to invest by way of mutual funds are interested in equity funds because of the potentially large returns they can earn from owning common stocks. Also, common stocks are relatively difficult securities to value, and many individual investors prefer to turn over to professional money managers the decisions regarding which stocks to buy and what prices to pay. What better way to obtain professional guidance than to have an investment manager assemble and manage your stock portfolio?

Fundamentals of Common Stocks

Shares of common stock represent units of ownership in a corporation. The more shares issued by a particular corporation, the smaller the proportional ownership a single share represents. If you own 100 shares of the stock of a company that has 10 million outstanding shares, you own 100/10,000,000, or .001 percent of the company. If you hold 100 shares of the stock of a company that has 1,000 outstanding shares, you own 10 percent of the company. The greater the percentage that you own of a company's stock, the more you influence the company's operations.

A company issues shares of common stock in order to

> Don't buy shares in a mutual fund until you first understand the investments the mutual fund holds in its portfolio.

raise capital to acquire buildings, purchase equipment, pay employees, buy materials, and so forth. In return for providing capital, common stockholders acquire an ownership interest in the company's assets and, more importantly, a claim to whatever income remains after all other obligations have been satisfied. Employees, suppliers, lenders, and state and local tax authorities all must be paid before a firm's stockholders have a claim to anything. Common stockholders have a residual claim to the revenues and assets that remain after all other parties have been paid.

The Value of Common Stock

Owners of common stock stand to benefit when a company's managers invest in assets that earn the firm substantial profits. If a company is able to utilize its assets to develop a widely needed drug, a highly efficient motor, a very comfortable and long-wearing shoe, or a more tasty ice cream, the company and its owners stand to gain great financial rewards. On the other hand, stockholders are likely to suffer financial losses when a firm's managers make poor use of the company's financial and physical resources. A series of investment blunders by a company may leave stockholders with nothing to share after all the company's other claimants have been paid.

The stockholders of a company can earn a return on their own investment in two ways: (1) from dividends that are periodically distributed to shareholders from the firm's profits, and (2) from increases in the market price of the firm's stock. Dividend distributions are determined by a company's directors who consider, among other things, the firm's need for expansion capital in relation to current profits. Companies that have only modest needs for additional assets often pay a large portion of their earnings in dividends. The directors of a rapidly growing company that requires large amounts of capital to pay for additional assets may decide to forego any dividend distribution to stockholders and retain all of the firm's profits for reinvestment. Companies that reinvest most or all of their earnings in additional assets cause their stockholders to sacrifice current dividend income in return for the likelihood of increased future profits.

The second potential source of stockholder income is an increase in the value of the stock owned. The term *potential* is appropriate because a stock's price *may* increase, but then again it may decline or not change in value at all. A stock price sometimes declines enough to more than offset dividend income, thereby causing a stockholder to suffer an overall loss.

A stock's price is influenced by many things, but none is more important than the investment community's expectations regarding the firm's *future* profits. An improved profit outlook will usually increase a firm's common stock price. Conversely, investors surprised by a company's announcement of a problem such as management turnover, plant closures, or falling sales are likely to revise their earnings forecasts downward and cause the firm's stock price to decline. Stock prices are also strongly influenced by interest rate changes. Rising interest rates tend to push stock prices downward while falling interest rates cause stock prices to rise.

Not all stock prices move together, even during major

movements in the overall stock market. For example, the common stocks of most utilities (electric companies, gas companies, telephone companies) are valued for stable earnings and dividends that cause the stocks' prices to be relatively stable compared to the overall stock market. Some stocks are strongly affected by interest rate movements while other stocks (e.g., defense firms, construction firms) are impacted more by government policy. Because stocks do not always move in tandem, the return you earn from common stocks is often as much a function of the particular stocks you own as of general stock market movements.

The Risks of Owning Common Stock

Common stock investments (and mutual funds that invest in common stocks) can produce impressive returns, but you also assume substantial risks by owning these financial assets. Common stocks are very difficult to value precisely because so many variables influence common stock prices. For example, your favorable impression of a company's product line may cause you to consider an investment in the firm's common stock. Further investigation of the company's financial statement indicates minimal debt and an impressive string of earnings increases. Everything seems to be in order. What you may not know is that a much larger firm is ready to introduce a competing product line of equal or better quality that will sell at a much lower price. Suddenly, a company with excellent prospects may turn into a business that has to fight for its survival. Owning shares of common stock is inherently risky because so many things can change the value of a company and its stock.

Stock prices tend to be very volatile, and the prices of

> Don't assume that your money is not at risk just because a mutual fund has professional portfolio management. Some mutual funds subject shareholders to substantial risk.

some stocks may bounce up or down by as much as 5 to 10 percent in a single day's trading. The stock prices of airline companies, automotive companies, and companies in many other cyclical industries are subject to major price swings that can cause large gains and losses for stockholders. Substantial price volatility is an important risk if you may have to liquidate an investment on short notice.

Stock price volatility stems in part from the fact that expectations regarding a company's future profits—the major variable influencing a company's stock price—are subject to constant and sudden revisions. Even relatively small changes in a company's revenues can cause major changes in the firm's profits. Unexpected changes in current earnings, in turn, can alarm investors who anticipated better results. Investors surprised by a decline in a company's reported earnings are likely to start selling the stock, driving the price down. Investors can be expected to buy the firm's common stock and drive its price up when earnings are higher than expected.

In the event a company runs into serious competitive, operational, or financial difficulties, causing its sales and profits to shrink, the firm's management may have to reduce or eliminate the dividend, an act that may precipitate a major decline in the common stock price. A company can lose money for only so long before it becomes unable even to pay its creditors. If a company encounters an unfavorable business environment for an extended period of time, its accumulated losses may be so great that the stockholders' investment is wiped out. The liquidation of a financially ailing company is one of the worst possible outcomes for the firm's stockholders, of course, but it can and does occur, especially in a weak economy.

Influences on Equity Fund Values

Chapter 2 discussed factors that influence the net asset value of a mutual fund's shares. At any particular time, an equity fund's overall value equals the cumulative value of the stocks owned (stock price times number of shares) plus the cash equivalents that are in the fund's portfolio awaiting investment. The net asset value of an equity fund is the current value of all the fund's assets divided by the fund's outstanding shares. Issuing additional shares of an equity fund causes no change in the fund's net asset value because the increase in the fund's assets is exactly offset by a proportional increase in the number of outstanding shares.

Changes in Net Asset Value

Changes in the prices of stocks held in a mutual fund's portfolio will change both the value of the fund's portfolio and, more importantly, the net asset value of the fund's shares. You can expect major upward movement in the stock market to be accompanied by an increase in the prices of most stocks held in a mutual fund's portfolio. An increase in a fund's assets caused by rising stock prices is independent of the outstanding shares and will cause an increase in the fund's net asset value. Likewise, a general downward move-

Figure 9

TEN LARGEST STOCK FUNDS, EARLY 1996

Fund Name	Assets (millions)	Sales Charge
Fidelity Magellan Fund	$55,502	3.00%
Investment Company of America	26,900	5.75
Vanguard Index 500	19,791	0
Washington Mutual Investors	19,786	5.75
Fidelity Growth & Income	16,906	3.00
Fidelity Puritan	16,430	0
Fidelity Contrafund	16,364	3.00
20th Century Ultra	16,186	0
Income Fund of America	14,329	5.75
Vanguard Windsor	13,997	0

ment in the stock market tends to cause a decline in the net asset value of an equity fund because the prices of stocks owned by the fund are likely to decline. In short, equity fund share prices (the net asset values) are driven by the prices of the common stocks these funds own.

Changes in an equity fund's net asset value depend both upon the particular stocks a fund owns and on movements in the stock market. If an equity fund owns the "right" stocks, the fund's net asset value will increase proportionately more than the overall stock market when the market is rising and will decrease proportionately less than the overall stock market when the market is falling. (The Standard & Poor's 500 Index is often used as a proxy for the overall stock market.) Unfortunately, the "right" stocks are very difficult to identify, even for professional portfolio managers.

Portfolio Management and Changes in Net Asset Value

Ideally, an equity fund manager will invest all the fund's assets in stocks that react strongly to overall market movements just prior to a major upward move in the market. Prior to a major dip in the market, the manager would alter the composition of the fund's portfolio by lightening up on stocks (i.e., decreasing the proportion of the fund's assets invested in stocks) and by moving into more conservative stocks. To accomplish this, a portfolio manager must be able to accurately forecast stock market movements, a task that many market researchers believe is, at best, very difficult.

In general, equity funds that hold nondiversified portfolios are subject to larger gains and losses in net asset values than funds that hold diversified portfolios. For example, equity funds that specialize in the common stocks of companies that operate in a particular industry or a particular country subject you to much greater risks than equity funds that hold a large variety of stocks because stocks of similar companies tend to move together. Unexpected events can strike an individual industry as well as an individual company.

Substantial research indicates that even professional portfolio managers have difficulty forecasting stock price movements with any degree of accuracy. Aggressive equity funds that outperform a rising stock market tend to underperform (show greater proportional losses) a falling stock

> You are likely to be best served by owning more than a single mutual fund. You may want to own several different types of funds including a money market fund, a fixed-income fund, and an equity fund.

market. Conservative equity funds that tend to underperform the market during a rising stock market generally outperform the market (show smaller proportional losses) during periods of falling stock prices. Most researchers who study the returns earned by mutual funds believe that the relative performance of an equity fund (i.e., the returns earned by a fund's shareholders compared to those returns earned by shareholders of other funds) in one year is of little or no value in forecasting the relative performance of the fund in the following year.

Types of Stock Funds

Stock funds are classified according to the investment objectives the funds pursue. Investment objectives determine the types of common stocks that equity funds hold in their portfolios. Mutual funds that seek to maximize capital growth invest in stocks that have the potential for achieving large price gains. Ownership of these same stocks nearly always entails substantial risks. The stocks of companies that can provide explosive growth nearly always carry some unwanted baggage: untried technology, recent rapid runups in the stock prices, high price-earnings ratios, uncertain markets, or the possibility of cutthroat competition.

You should strive to select a fund with an investment objective that is compatible with your own investment goals. Just as a young single person or a middle-aged couple is unlikely to want to invest all of their money in a fund that provides mostly current dividend income, a retired couple is unlikely to want a substantial portion of their money invested in an aggressive growth fund.

Some financial advisers suggest that you spread your money among a number of different funds with different investment goals. For example, you might want to invest in both an equity-income fund and a growth fund. Always remember that it is wise to hedge your bets. No matter how strongly you believe stocks are headed for a major bull market, you may be wrong. Just as the three most important determinants of real estate value are location, location, and location, the three most important words of advice in stock market investing are diversify, diversify, and diversify.

The major types of equity funds and a short description of each follow.

Aggressive growth funds concentrate their investments in the common stocks of small, growing companies with the potential to produce substantial gains for stockholders. These small companies generally do not pay dividends, so that aggressive growth funds provide little, if any, regular income to their shareholders. Aggressive growth funds tend to show large gains in net asset value during rising markets and large losses in net asset value during major market declines. The high price volatility and lack of regular income subjects shareholders of aggressive growth funds to substantial amounts of risk. These funds are not for the faint of heart.

Balanced funds hold portfolios comprised of common stocks, preferred stocks, and bonds. Balanced funds seek a compromise between current income and growth by investing in a combination of securities that provides some income and the possibility for some growth. Common stocks provide the potential of an increase in net asset value at the same time that interest from bonds and dividends from preferred stocks allow a balanced fund to pay a moderate dividend to its shareholders. Balanced funds generally underperform a

> Specialized sector funds pose great risks and should be selected with care.

strong stock market and outperform a weak stock market. Shares in balanced funds are suitable for relatively conservative investors.

Global equity funds invest in the common stocks of foreign companies as well as the common stocks of U.S. companies. Global funds allow investors to participate in the ownership of foreign companies that may have superior growth prospects compared to many domestic companies. Shares traded in foreign securities markets are denominated in foreign currencies, causing the returns of a global fund to be influenced both by changes in the market values of the stocks (as denominated in each stock's respective currency) *and* by the rate at which the foreign currencies can be exchanged for dollars. A global equity fund is negatively affected by a strengthening U.S. dollar and positively affected by a weakening U.S. dollar.

Growth funds are the most popular type of equity fund. Growth funds acquire the common stocks of relatively large and well-known companies that offer the potential for substantial growth in earnings and dividends. Growth funds generally provide only modest amounts of current dividend income because they invest in the stocks of companies that retain and reinvest most of their profits. Although growth funds invest in the stocks of companies that portfolio managers believe will produce long-term price appreciation, these funds tend to avoid the high-risk stocks favored by aggressive growth funds. Growth funds are especially suitable for young and middle-aged investors who have a long investment horizon.

Growth and income funds invest in common stocks that offer good possibilities for growing revenues and profits but also pay relatively high dividends. These funds tend to buy the stocks of mature companies that still have the potential for growing revenues and earnings. Growth and income funds hold fairly conservative portfolios that provide less growth than growth funds and less income than funds that concentrate on high-dividend stocks.

Income-equity funds attempt to provide shareholders with a high level of current income by investing in common stocks that pay dividends that are relatively large compared to the respective stock prices. Common stocks with large dividend returns that are owned by income-equity funds generally have a limited potential for capital gains. Thus, you should purchase income-equity funds if you are more interested in current income than in capital growth. The net asset values of income-equity funds are heavily influenced by movements in long-term interest rates. The NAVs of these funds tend to increase when interest rates decline.

Index funds assemble portfolios that attempt to match the returns of the overall stock market as measured by a particular index, generally the Standard & Poor's 500. The philosophy of an index fund is that mutual funds have historically had a difficult time consistently outperforming the market, so why try? An index fund minimizes the expenses of research and trading by assembling and maintaining a portfolio that emulates the market. Index funds generally have the lowest expenses of any equity funds. Because the Standard & Poor's 500 is heavily weighted with blue chip stocks, index funds tend to be conservative funds that out-

> Unusually good investment performance during a bull market by a mutual fund is often the result of the fund owning a portfolio of high-risk securities. Beware of buying shares of a mutual fund based solely on the fund's investment performance during one part of a stock market cycle.

perform income funds but underperform growth funds during strong stock markets.

International funds invest in the common stocks of companies located outside the United States. These funds allow investors to own the common stocks of foreign companies without the hassle of exchanging currencies or paying unusually high commissions. Like global funds, international funds allow you to earn returns based on a combination of (1) the returns provided by the portfolio's stocks in the countries in which they are traded, and (2) the rate at which the foreign currencies exchange for the dollar. For example, an international fund may own several German stocks that are increasing in price in terms of the German marks in which they are traded, but the fund may still lose money on the investment because of declines in the German mark relative to the dollar. An increase in the value of the mark can cause the net asset value of an international fund to increase even though the market values of its German stocks decline somewhat.

Option-income funds attempt to increase the current income of shareholders by investing in dividend-paying common stocks and *writing* (selling short) *call options* that generate premium income. A *call option* gives its owner the right, but not the obligation, to buy shares of stock at a fixed price until an agreed-upon date. Writing options causes the mutual fund to surrender the chance to earn large capital gains on the stock it owns in return for fees (termed *premiums*) the fund receives from the option buyers. The complicated transactions of option-income funds generally produce greater-than-average expenses and frequent trades that result in large brokerage fees. Option-income funds produce the best relative results when the stock market makes small up-and-down movements but mainly moves sideways.

Precious metals funds invest in the common stocks of companies engaged in businesses associated with the mining and sale of gold, silver, and other precious metals. The profitability of owning these funds depends on the prices of precious metals. If gold and silver prices rise, as would be likely during inflationary times or periods of international turmoil, owning precious metals funds should provide superior investment results. These funds are likely to underperform the overall stock market during periods of economic growth unless the growth is accompanied by increased inflationary expectations. Some financial experts advise that investors keep at least a small portion of their portfolio in precious metals or the stocks of precious metals companies.

Sector funds invest in the common stocks of a single industry. For example, a particular sector fund might invest only in the stocks of companies engaged in telecommunications. Unlike the majority of equity funds that reduce risk by diversifying their portfolios across a large number of industries, sector funds attract investors who seek to limit their investment to a particular industry but not a particular company. The lack of diversification causes sector funds to produce very large gains in some years and very large losses in other years. Sector funds have great price volatility, and you should purchase them only if you are willing to assume large risks.

CHAPTER 4

Bond Funds

Bond funds invest their shareholders' money in the bonds of corporations and governmental organizations. These funds are purchased by investors who seek conservative investments that pay relatively high current income. The values of bond funds, especially funds that own bonds with long maturities, are primarily driven by interest rates. The net asset values of bond funds move inversely with interest rates. In general, bond funds are subject to smaller variations in price than are equity funds.

Mutual funds that specialize in bond investments came of age in the mid-1980s as investors chased the high current returns offered by corporate and government bonds. Net assets in bond and income funds virtually exploded from $54 billion in 1984 to $684 billion only a decade later (see Figure 10). Although bonds are generally easier to value than

Figure 10

ASSETS MANAGED BY BOND AND INCOME FUNDS

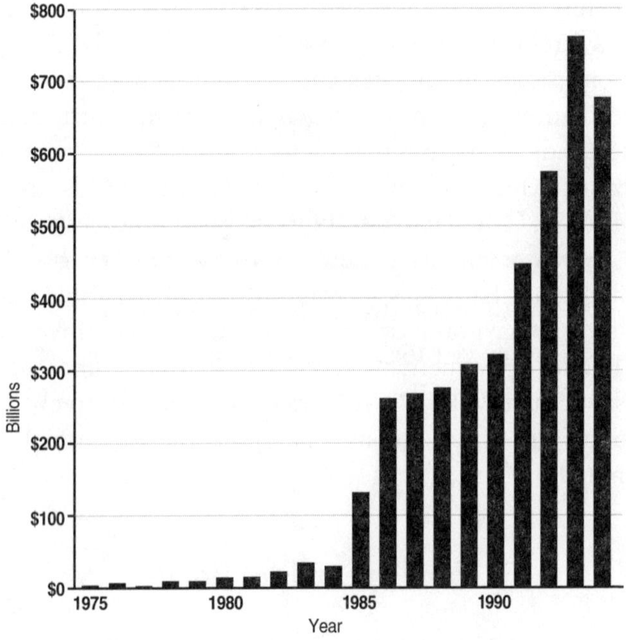

Source: Investment Company Institute, *Mutual Fund Fact Book*

common stocks, a diversified portfolio of individual bond issues requires a substantial investment of money, so many individuals find it more convenient and affordable to invest in the shares of bond funds than to purchase individual bond issues.

Bond funds are ongoing companies that continually reinvest the proceeds from securities that are sold or redeemed. Continuous reinvestment of the proceeds from security sales means there is no specific date on which shareholders in a bond fund are scheduled to have their money returned as would occur if individual bond issues were owned. Bonds mature, but bond funds do not. Only the bonds owned by bond funds mature, and the money received from matured bonds is reinvested in other bonds.

Bond funds pay higher current returns and vary less in price than equity funds. The higher current return paid by bond funds is the result of higher current yields from bond interest payments compared to the dividend yields on common stocks. The relative stability of bond fund net asset values results from the general price stability of bonds. A mutual fund that owns securities that exhibit stable market prices will have a stable net asset value. The investment goals and investment performance of bond funds attract mostly conservative investors who seek relatively large amounts of current income. The potential for capital gains is limited.

Fundamentals of Bonds

A bond is evidence of debt on the part of the security's issuer. Investors who purchase bonds become creditors of the

> Keep accurate and complete records of security transactions. You will need them for calculating your income taxes.

organization that issued the bonds. Bonds have a stated maturity on which the principal amount owed on the debt is scheduled for full repayment. Between the time bonds are issued and the time they are redeemed, the issuer is generally required to make a series of fixed semiannual interest payments, in amounts determined by the stated interest rate (called the *coupon* or *coupon rate*) and the principal amount of the debt. For example, a 7-percent coupon, $1,000-par bond (a bond that can be collected for its face value of $1,000) requires the issuer to pay $70 in annual interest (7 percent of $1,000) for each outstanding bond. Each year's payments are made in two installments of $35 each for as long as the bond is outstanding. A 9-percent coupon, $1,000 principal amount bond will pay annual interest of $90 in the form of two $45 payments.

Corporate bonds are nearly always denominated in $1,000 amounts while bonds issued by cities and states (termed *municipal bonds*) are generally denominated in $5,000 amounts. The owner of a $5,000 principal amount, 6-percent coupon municipal bond will receive $300 of annual interest. U.S. government securities are issued in various denominations depending upon the particular type of bond. Treasury bills (U.S. Treasury securities with original maturities of one year or less) are denominated in $10,000 amounts while long-term Treasury bonds are denominated in $1,000 amounts. Federal agency securities are issued in $5,000 denominations.

Organizations borrow money for many reasons. Corporations issue bonds in order to obtain money to acquire additional assets or to pay off outstanding debt. Bond issues are an alternative to diluting ownership by selling more shares of common stock. Governments issue bonds when tax revenues are insufficient to cover spending. The federal government annually borrows hundreds of billions of dollars to pay for spending that is in excess of its tax revenues. Likewise, cities and states issue bonds to pay for parks, bridges, water systems, rapid transit systems, stadiums, and a variety of other needs. The federal government and state and local governments also issue bonds in order to raise the money to pay off outstanding bonds that reach maturity.

Bonds create a legal obligation on the part of a borrower to make the specified interest payments and to repay the debt's principal amount at maturity. Interest and principal payments on corporate debt have priority over payments of any kind to a firm's stockholders. Payments to creditors must be made in full and on time, or legal action is likely to be initiated by the creditors. In contrast, payments to a company's shareholders are at the discretion of a firm's directors. The priority debt enjoys over equity allows bondholders more confidence than stockholders regarding how much money they will receive and when they will be paid.

How Bonds Are Valued

A bond is valued for the cash payments of interest and principal that are promised to the bondholder. A bond is more valuable the higher its interest payments, the greater the size of the principal repayment, and the greater the certainty that these payments will be made in full and on schedule. A bond's value is also influenced by the length of time before

Figure 11

BOND CREDIT RATINGS AND THEIR MEANINGS

Standard & Poor's	Moody's	Meaning
AAA	Aaa	High-grade with strong capacity for repayment
AA	Aa	High-grade but slightly lower margins of protection
A	A	Medium grade with favorable attributes but susceptibility to adverse economic conditions
BBB	Baa	Medium grade but lacking certain protection against adverse economic conditions
BB	Ba	Speculative with moderate protection in an unstable economy
B	B	Speculative with small assurance of principal and interest
CCC	Caa	Poor quality in default or in danger of default
CC	Ca	Highly speculative
C		Extremely poor investment quality
	C	Making no interest payments
D		Default with interest in arrears

the debt is scheduled to be repaid by the borrower. The degree to which maturity length influences a bond's price depends upon how the bond's coupon rate compares to the current market rate of interest on bonds of similar risk and maturity.

Both the credit worthiness of the issuer and the specific assets (if any) that are pledged as collateral affect a bond's credit quality. A bond with the weak guarantee of a company that is encountering substantial financial difficulties is likely to have its price penalized by investors unless the bond carries a relatively high coupon rate. Investors who prefer high-quality bonds that are certain to be repaid must be willing to accept a reduced amount of interest income in order to own these securities.

Bond investors generally rely on credit ratings supplied by several private rating agencies that are in the business of judging a borrower's credit worthiness. These agencies consider management quality, profitability, revenue forecasts, existing interest obligations, and many other factors when they develop a bond issue's quality rating. Ratings supplied by the rating agencies play a major role in determining the interest rate a borrower must pay in order to sell bonds to investors.

Bond values are primarily affected by changes in market rates of interest. Rising interest rates cause a decline in the prices of outstanding bonds, and falling interest rates cause these same bonds to increase in price. Suppose in 1986 you purchased a $10,000 principal amount bond with a 10-percent coupon and a 2010 maturity. You have received $1,000 (10 percent of $10,000) of annual interest from the issuer of the bond since 1986. Now, ten years following the issue date, market interest rates have declined, and newly issued bonds similar to the bond you own carry a coupon rate of only 7 percent. Buyers of these new bonds will receive $70 in annual interest per $1,000 principal amount compared to the $100 per bond that you continue to receive. Even though market rates of interest have changed, the coupon rate on your bond is fixed, and your semiannual interest payments remain unchanged. The bonds you own pay a greater amount of annual interest and will be worth substantially more than newly issued bonds.

The degree to which a bond will sell at a premium or a discount to par value is influenced by the length of time before the bond matures. A bond with a relatively high coupon rate will sell at a larger premium to par value when the bond has a long maturity because above-average interest payments will occur for many years. A bond with an above-market coupon rate is more valuable the longer the time before the bond is scheduled for redemption. Conversely, a bond with a below-market coupon rate is less valuable the longer the time to maturity.

The sooner a bond's principal is to be repaid, the more closely a bond will sell to its face value. A $1,000 par value bond that is one month from maturity will sell for approximately $1,000 regardless of the bond's coupon rate and the market rate of interest because the face amount of the bond will soon be returned to the bondholder. A bond that is many years from being redeemed may sell at either a large premium or a large discount to its principal amount.

The Risks of Owning Bonds

Bonds are generally less risky to own than common stocks. A bondholder knows exactly how much money to expect and on what dates money will be received. Compared to a

> Avoid tax-exempt bond and money market funds unless you pay federal income taxes at a rate of 28 percent or above.

bondholder, a stockholder has less certainty both about dividends and about the future value of the stock. Bondholders are uncertain of the cash payments they will receive only when there is a possibility the bonds may have to be sold prior to maturity or when there is a question about the credit quality of the issuer. Both these uncertainties can be avoided by selecting high-quality bonds with appropriate maturities.

An important risk faced by owners of long-term bonds is the possibility that inflation will eat away at the purchasing power of bond payments. The fixed payments stipulated by bonds hold advantages for a bondholder, but they also create a situation in which persistent inflation will eat away at the real value of each payment. By the time a bond's principal is returned at maturity, a bondholder may find that a current dollar is worth less than 50 cents compared to the dollars originally used to buy the bond. A long period of high inflation may cause bond payments to be worth only pennies on the dollar. The longer a bond's maturity, the greater the risk that unanticipated inflation will drastically reduce the purchasing power of a bond's investment income.

Most bonds subject a bondholder to the risk that not all the promised payments will be made by the bond's issuer. Companies that appear to be financially healthy can run into any number of unexpected problems that can leave them unable to service their debt. Times change, and products go out of style at the same time that new competitors attempt to eat away at a firm's market share. Companies will sometimes become overly aggressive in the financing they employ. The 1980s witnessed company after company undertaking substantial borrowing in order to improve the returns earned by their stockholders. In some instances, even healthy companies ended up unable to meet the monumental interest and principal obligations of the added borrowing. Investors who had purchased what was once considered high-quality debt were left holding bonds of questionable value.

Many long-term corporate bonds are subject to early redemption (redemption prior to the scheduled maturity) at a fixed price. Early redemptions are most likely to occur following a period of falling interest rates because borrowers would like to replace their old high-interest debt with newly issued debt at a lower interest rate. The possibility of an early redemption is a serious risk to owners of bonds that can be called away by issuers because the redemption is likely to occur at the worst possible time—a period when the principal returned will be reinvested at a relatively low rate of interest. Before purchasing a bond you should *always* determine if the bond is subject to early redemption, especially if the bond sells at a premium to par.

Influences on Bond Fund Values

Changes in the net asset values of bond funds result from changes in the market values of the bonds these funds hold

> Most individuals should have at least some of their portfolio in equities or in mutual funds that own equities.

Figure 12

MATURITY LENGTH AND CHANGES IN BOND PRICES

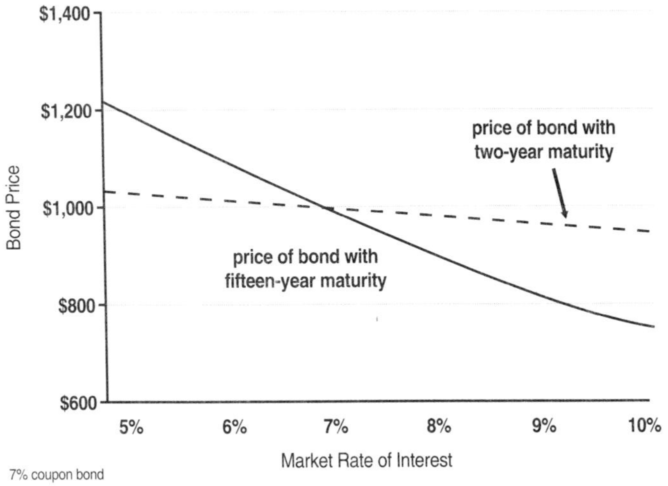

in their portfolios. Thus, changes in the NAVs of bond funds are mostly caused by changes in market interest rates. An increase in market interest rates will cause a decline in the net asset values of bond funds because there will be a decline in the market values of the bonds these funds are holding. Interest rate changes drive bond values that comprise the portfolios of bond funds.

The extent to which a bond fund's NAV is influenced by changes in interest rates depends on the maturity lengths of the bonds the fund holds in its portfolio. The longer the average maturity of the bonds owned, the more the net asset value of the fund is affected by changing interest rates. Mutual funds that invest in long-term bonds subject their shareholders to a greater variation in share prices than do mutual funds that invest in bonds with intermediate or short maturities.

The net asset values of bond funds are affected to a lesser extent by the quality of the bonds owned. A bond fund that holds mostly low-quality bonds (also called *junk bonds*) may experience reductions in NAV during periods of economic decline when investors tend to shy away from risky investments. Some borrowers may cease interest payments during an extended period of economic weakness, causing a major decline in the market values of the firms' bonds and a substantial erosion in the net asset values of funds that hold these bonds.

Types of Long-Term Bond Funds

Although all bonds are not alike, the variety of bonds is considerably smaller than the variety of common stocks. Bonds differ mainly by coupon rate, redemption date, credit quality, and type of issuer. With relatively few major differences in all of the thousands of outstanding bond issues, there are a limited number of ways for a bond fund to differentiate itself from the hundreds of other bond funds in existence.

One important difference between bond funds is the average maturity length of the portfolios. Bond funds that invest in long-term bonds offer higher current yields and greater NAV volatility than bond funds that invest in short-term bonds. Bond funds that invest in short-term bonds generally offer relatively low current yields but little volatility in NAV. When you invest in a mutual fund that owns a portfolio of short-term bonds, you can generally count on being able to liquidate your shares at a price close to what you paid.

The major types of bond funds are listed below.

Corporate bond funds invest in bonds issued by corporations. These funds pay dividends to shareholders that are taxable by both federal and state authorities. Some corporate bond funds concentrate on bonds with long maturities while other funds hold bonds of intermediate length. In general, corporate bond funds pay a higher current return than bond funds that invest in government bonds or municipal bonds.

GNMA (Ginnie Mae) funds invest in mortgage-backed securities (i.e., real estate loans) of the Government National Mortgage Association. Principal and interest payments on Ginnie Mae securities originate from the mortgage payments made by homeowners. The Ginnie Mae payments are guaranteed by the U.S. government. Ginnie Mae funds offer relatively high current returns, although there is substantial uncertainty about when principal will be repaid. Even though the payments on Ginnie Mae securities are guaranteed, these securities change in market value in response to changes in interest rates.

Global bond funds invest in bonds issued in various countries including the United States. Being able to invest overseas allows a portfolio manager to search the world for bonds that offer the best interest rates. The interest payments earned by owners of a global bond fund depend upon the interest earned on the bonds that are held (in the respective foreign currency) and on the rate at which the respective currencies exchange for dollars. Interest earned in foreign currencies must be exchanged for dollars before dividends can be paid to shareholders. Likewise, the net asset values of global bond funds depend on the bond prices as denominated in the currencies of the countries in which the bonds are issued and on the respective rates at which these currencies exchange for dollars. Global bond funds offer both added opportunities and added risks compared to funds that restrict their investments to domestic bonds.

High-yield bond funds, also called *junk bond funds*, invest in low-rated bonds that offer above-average yields. The investment philosophy of high-yield bond funds is to accept extra risk in order to earn a higher return for their shareholders. High-yield bond funds do provide higher current returns compared to other bond funds, but at the risk of greater price volatility and a greater likelihood that the issuers of some of the bonds held by the funds may default on their obligation to pay interest and principal. Defaults will reduce the yields and possibly the net asset values of the funds. High-yield bond funds are for investors who consider themselves to be risk takers.

Income bond funds invest in a mix of corporate and government bonds in order to earn high current income for the funds' shareholders. Income bond funds have the flexibility to alter the maturity lengths of their portfolios and to move between corporate bonds and government bonds in order to take advantage of interest rate differences. For example, an income bond fund might move most of its portfolio into corporate bonds at a time when these securities offer an unusually high interest premium over government bonds.

Municipal bond funds invest in the bonds of states, cities, and political subdivisions in order to earn tax-exempt in-

> Beware of investing in a mutual fund with unusually high turnover of its portfolio. Frequent trading can be costly and reduce the returns you earn as a shareholder.

come for shareholders. Most municipal bond funds collect tax-exempt interest and pass along tax-exempt dividends to the funds' shareholders. Municipal bond funds are of interest to investors who have substantial taxable income that causes them to pay relatively high income tax rates. Some municipal bond funds specialize in the bonds of a particular state (sometimes called *single state funds*) in order to pay dividends that are exempt from state and local taxes as well as from federal income taxes. Municiapl bond funds also sometimes concentrate their portfolios in municipal bonds of certain quality categories.

U.S. government income funds invest in debt securities of the U.S. government. Most government bond funds invest in a variety of government bonds, including U.S. Treasury obligations and the bonds of federal agencies such as the Federal National Mortgage Association and the Federal Home Loan Bank. Federal agency bonds entail slightly more risk, and pay slightly higher interest rates, than direct obligations of the U.S. Treasury. U.S. government income funds pay dividends that are taxable by the federal government but generally free of taxation by state and local governments. Some of these funds limit their investments to direct obligations of the U.S. Treasury.

CHAPTER 5

Money Market Funds

Money market funds are specialized mutual funds that restrict their investments to very short-term debt securities. These funds offer stable share values and great liquidity, but only modest yields. Money market funds are generally used as substitutes for savings accounts and money market deposit accounts. Although not insured, most money market funds offer a high degree of safety with regard to the principal that is invested. Many funds limit their investments to short-term state and local debt and pay a dividend that is exempt from federal income taxes.

Although money market mutual funds serve a very different investment function than the equity funds and bond funds discussed in chapters 3 and 4, all three types of funds have the same organizational structure. Like equity and bond funds, a money market fund continually issues and redeems shares in response to changes in investor demand. The identifying feature of money market funds is a portfolio of very short-term debt instruments. Limiting investments to very short-term debt results in these funds having stable share values but relatively low returns. The stable value of short-term debt securities allows money market mutual funds to stabilize the value of their own shares. The stable value of the shares, in turn, protects shareholders of money market mutual funds from the major risk of owning equity funds and bond funds: volatility of net asset value.

The Stability of Money Market Fund Share Values

The market values of all negotiable interest-bearing securities are affected to some degree by changing market rates of interest, but securities with maturity lengths of less than a year are affected relatively little. Even large variations in market interest rates have only a small effect on the price of a Treasury bill or negotiable certificate of deposit scheduled to mature and repay its face amount in a matter of weeks. A Treasury bill that is scheduled to return its face value of $10,000 in a month can be sold to another investor for near the face value regardless of the level of interest rates. Because a mutual fund's net asset value is a direct function of the value of the fund's assets, stable asset values result in a stable net asset value for the fund's shares. Money market

> Stay informed. The more you understand about business and financial matters, the better investment decisions you are likely to make.

securities owned by these funds generally have very active secondary markets and are easily bought and sold without any effect on their market values. Thus, a money market fund that is hit with large shareholder redemptions can easily liquidate a substantial portion of its portfolio at near to face value.

The combination of liquidity and stable security values enables money market funds to stabilize the net asset value of their shares at $1, thus permitting investors to buy and redeem shares at a fixed price. Assets can be readily sold at a known price when shareholders redeem shares, and additional securities are easily purchased when a fund receives additional shareholder money. Being able to redeem shares at a fixed value is a shareholder luxury that money market funds, but not equity or bond funds, are able to provide.

Be warned that money market funds do not guarantee that the price of their shares will *always* be $1. In a few instances, a portion of the investments held by a money market fund have declined in value to such an extent that the fund's managers could not maintain the $1 share price. Rather than suffer the bad publicity that would ensue, the fund sponsors generally maintained the $1 price by pumping additional money into the fund. This drastic step was not legally required of the sponsors; shareholders could have found themselves holding shares with a value of less than $1. The ability of a fund's managers to maintain a stable share price depends on the maturity length, quality, and liquidity of securities held by the fund. Reaching for higher yields by purchasing securities with increased maturities, lower quality, and reduced liquidity can pose risks for shareholders.

Investments Held by Money Market Mutual Funds

Money market funds invest in corporate and government debt securities with very short maturities. The Securities and Exchange Commission requires that these funds maintain portfolios with average maturities of 90 days or less. At year-end 1994, taxable money market funds held assets with an average maturity of 34 days. The portfolio of a money market fund is likely to contain Treasury bills, other short-term government securities, repurchase agreements (also called *repos*, these loans use U.S. government securities as collateral), certificates of deposit (CDs) issued by commercial banks and savings and loans, commercial paper (short-term corporate IOUs), and bankers' acceptances (short-term credit instruments guaranteed by commercial banks). Some money market funds also invest in Eurodollar CDs. As a general rule, money market funds restrict their investments to high-quality securities that are easily bought and sold. The Securities and Exchange Commission requires that money market funds invest only in investment-quality commercial paper. The SEC also restricts taxable money market funds from investing more than 5 percent of their assets in the securities of any one issuer.

Even though money market funds generally hold high-quality debt instruments, not all the investments purchased by these funds are of equal quality. Just as important is the fact that not all money market funds hold these securities in

Figure 13

TYPICAL ASSET MIX OF
TAXABLE MONEY MARKET FUNDS

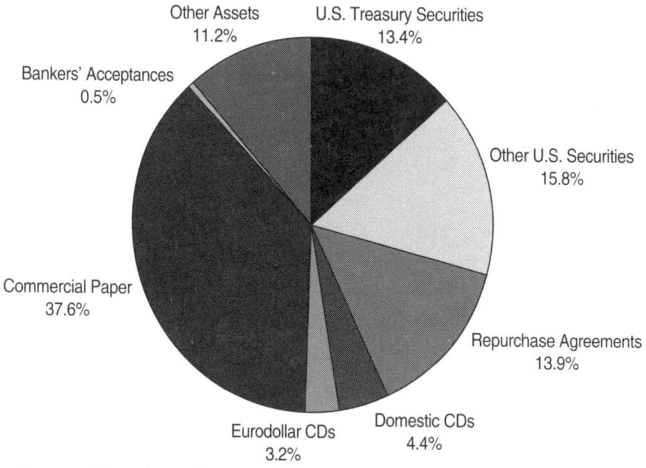

Source: *Mutual Fund Fact Book*

equal proportion. Money market funds compete for investors primarily via the yields they offer. Funds that provide the highest yields are likely to capture the greatest amount of new investor money. One method used by some money market fund portfolio managers in order to offer higher yields is to purchase some riskier securities that have relatively high yields. For example, money market portfolio managers sometimes include securities backed by auto loans and credit-card receivables in their portfolios. A manager may increase the portfolio's yield by including certificates of deposit from financially shaky commercial banks that must pay high interest rates to attract capital. Complicated new securities with floating yields pegged to foreign currencies have also been developed and marketed to money market managers. Likewise, some money market funds are increasingly substituting slightly riskier federal agency issues for direct obligations of the U.S. government. If a borrower defaults on a security held in a money market fund's portfolio, the fund will be stuck with a security of questionable value and the fund's shareholders will observe either a decline in the fund's net asset value or a reduction in the yield.

Types of Money Market Funds

Money market funds are primarily differentiated on the basis of the tax status of the securities held in their portfolios. The majority of money market funds invest in taxable securities, such as short-term U.S. Treasury securities and certificates of deposit, and pay taxable dividends to their shareholders. A smaller but increasing number of money market funds invest in short-term tax-exempt securities and pay their shareholders tax- exempt dividends (at the federal level). Some money market funds restrict their investments to tax-exempt money market securities from a particular state so that the funds' dividends are exempt from state and local taxes as well as from federal income taxes.

Money market funds that restrict their investments to short-term U.S. government securities gained popularity in the late 1980s and early 1990s when investors became concerned about the increasing number of business bankruptcies and weaknesses in the U.S. financial system. Some funds restrict their investments to direct obligations of the U.S. Treasury in an effort to provide investors with the safest possible portfolio of short-term securities. Investors who re-

Figure 14

ASSETS MANAGED BY TAXABLE AND TAX-EXEMPT MONEY MARKET FUNDS

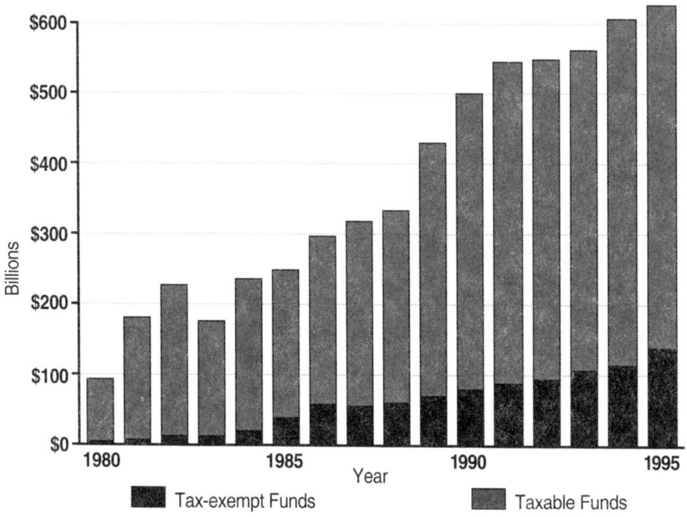

Source: Investment Company Institute, *Mutual Fund Fact Book*

side in states with high income tax rates benefit most from owning money market funds that invest in U.S. government securities because these funds pay dividends that generally escape taxation by state and local authorities (although not the higher rate levied by federal authorities).

Shareholder Expenses Associated with Money Market Funds

Money market funds, even those sold by brokerage firms, do not charge the sales or redemption fees that are common

Expense ratios and 12b–1 fees should be important considerations in selecting money market funds and bond funds that are desirable mostly for the current income they provide.

with equity and bond funds. Like these other funds, money market funds do levy an annual fee to cover their operating and portfolio management expenses. Some funds annually charge as little as .3 percent of the funds' average assets to pay for operating expenses while other funds charge nearly twice this rate. Differences in expense ratios among different funds have a direct effect on the yields earned by their shareholders. The differences are especially evident in the yields stockholders receive during periods of low interest rates. When money market funds are earning as little as 3 to 4 percent on short-term debt instruments, an extra annual expense of .2 or .3 percent makes an important difference in the return a money market shareholder earns.

Some money market funds charge a separate 12b-1 fee to pay for distribution costs, sometimes including payment to salespeople who sell the funds. These fees, which result in a direct reduction in the yield earned by shareholders, are most prevalent among money market funds sold through brokerage firms. It is to your advantage to avoid money market funds that charge a 12b–1 distribution fee.

Using Money Market Funds

Money market funds serve both as a place to temporarily park idle money that you soon expect to use and as a place to permanently keep some money that you may need on short notice. For example, a money market fund is useful when you want to set aside money to pay for an upcoming major expenditure or for an investment you anticipate making. You might place the proceeds from a security sale in a money market fund when no acceptable reinvestment alternatives are available. You can also use a money market fund to accumulate savings that will be used within a year or two to pay for expensive purchases such as a new car or major vacation. Money market mutual funds offer flexibility because you can add to your account whenever you like and you can withdraw funds without penalty whenever the need arises. Money market funds are excellent places to stash money for possible emergencies because of the liquidity and safety they offer.

Choosing between a taxable and tax-free money market fund should be determined by the after-tax rate of return you will earn from each investment. The after-tax return is a function of both your marginal tax rate and the difference in yields available on taxable and tax-exempt funds. The smaller the difference between the two yields, the more likely it is that you will benefit from choosing a tax-exempt fund. It is generally advantageous to stick with a taxable fund unless your federal tax rate is 28 percent or above, although you can be certain only after calculating the after-tax return for each alternative. Residing in a high-tax state such as California or New York may make it desirable to invest in a tax-exempt money market fund that specializes in tax-exempt securities of the state in which you live.

CHAPTER 6

Buying and Selling Mutual Funds

Mutual funds use several methods to distribute their shares to investors. Most funds sell their shares through either a captive or an independent sales force. Other funds choose to sell their shares directly to investors. Purchasing mutual fund shares from a salesperson normally involves some type of fee while shares purchased from a fund that sells directly often do not require either a sales fee or a redemption fee. Money market mutual funds do not charge sales or redemption fees. A mutual fund's fee schedule and the methods it uses to distribute and redeem its shares are spelled out in the fund's prospectus.

If you decide to purchase shares of common stock in Goodyear or you want to acquire $10,000 face amount of bonds issued by the city of Rushville, Indiana, you have little choice but to employ the services of a brokerage firm that will charge a commission when the order is executed. You will also have to go through a brokerage firm and pay a commission to sell bonds or shares of stock that you own. Only a limited number of companies sell shares of their own common stock directly to investors, and no firms offer to buy back their shares on demand. All brokerage companies have access to virtually the same wide range of secondary markets.

Mutual fund shares are bought and sold differently from negotiable securities even though mutual funds are corporate shells that hold negotiable securities. The shares of many mutual funds are purchased through sales organizations authorized by the funds' sponsors to sell and redeem the shares. Shares of other mutual funds can only be purchased from the funds themselves. Mutual funds that operate without the assistance of a sales force must rely on advertising, investment performance, and word of mouth to create investor demand for their shares.

Whether you purchase shares from a salesperson or directly from the fund, the shares you buy will be issued by the fund and will not come from another investor as is generally the case when you buy individual stocks and bonds. Mutual fund shares are issued to you by the fund's underwriter even when you purchase the shares through a salesperson. Likewise, shares redeemed through an agent will be returned to

> Periodically reevaluate your investment goals to determine if you should alter the allocation of your investments.

the fund's underwriter for redemption rather than sold to another investor.

How Mutual Funds Distribute their Shares

A mutual fund employs one of three methods to distribute its shares to investors. Many funds eliminate the need for a sales force by selling their shares directly to the public. These funds appeal to investors who want to avoid dealing with a salesperson and paying a sales commission. Other funds believe their shares can best be promoted by a sales force. Funds that use salespeople to distribute their shares either employ their own sales forces or use the sales staffs of other organizations. Each of the three distribution methods has advantages and disadvantages, both for the fund and for individuals who invest in it. A mutual fund's policy regarding the sale and redemption of its shares is spelled out in the fund's prospectus, a legal document that is discussed in greater detail in the following chapter.

Most mutual funds require a minimum initial investment when you open an account. The minimum varies from one fund to the next, but it is typically $500, $1,000, or $2,500, with bond funds generally requiring larger minimums than stock funds, and funds sold directly requiring higher minimums than funds sold through a sales force. The minimums are often reduced when mutual fund shares are used in a retirement plan or when an investor enters into a contract to make regular purchases. Some funds also establish minimums on subsequent investments to an account, but the required amounts are generally quite small, sometimes only $25 or $50.

Figure 15

MINIMUM INVESTMENTS REQUIRED
BY SELECTED MUTUAL FUNDS

Fund	Initial Investment	Subsequent Investment
Dreyfus Balanced Fund	$ 2,500	$ 100
Eaton Vance Tax Free Reserves	1,000	50
Evergreen Fund	2,000	0
Fidelity Global Bond Fund	2,500	250
Franklin Strategic Income Fund	100	25
Gabelli Growth Fund	1,000	0
Janus Fund	1,000	50
Keystone Tax-Free Fund	10,000	0
Monitor Income Equity Fund	1,000	500
PaineWebber Municipal High Income Fund	1,000	100
Sentry Fund	500	20
Strong Investment Fund	250	50
Vanguard/Windsor II Fund	3,000	100

Some mutual funds, including most large funds, offer special programs for share purchases. For example, a mutual fund may offer an accumulation plan in which you agree to periodically purchase shares of the fund. Payment for purchases may be made through payroll deductions or through automatic debiting of your bank account. Some accumulation plans allow substantial flexibility in the amounts you are permitted to invest while other plans involve a firm commitment.

Distribution through a Sales Force

Many investment companies distribute their shares by establishing sales agreements with independent agents. An insurance agency, a brokerage firm, or a financial planner may serve as an agent for several mutual fund sponsors. A second group of sponsors distribute their funds through their own sales organizations. Many large insurance companies and brokerage firms that sponsor and manage mutual funds have their own captive sales organizations to distribute the funds. These organizations may also sell the mutual funds of other sponsors.

Not all mutual funds that distribute their shares by means of a sales force can be purchased at every brokerage company or through every sales organization. Each brokerage company, insurance agent, and financial planner handles mutual funds from a limited number of sponsors with which it has a sales agreement. However, any sales organization is likely to offer enough variety that you will be able to choose among funds with a wide selection of investment objectives. If you are more interested in choosing a fund with a particular investment objective (e.g., aggressive growth, high current income, or tax-exempt income) than in owning the shares of a particular fund, nearly any broker or financial planner will offer one or more funds that meet your needs. However, if you want to purchase shares of a particular mutual fund, you may have to contact several brokerage firms before you locate one authorized to sell shares of that fund. Alternatively, you can contact the mutual fund and inquire about buying the shares directly or ask what companies are authorized to sell the firm's shares.

Many mutual funds that distribute their shares through a

sales force are sponsored by individual brokerage companies that sell the funds. Most large retail broker-dealers sponsor and sell a variety of their own mutual funds as well as funds from other sponsors. Shares of an *in-house* or *proprietary fund* can normally only be bought and sold through the firm that sponsors the fund. For example, you can buy and sell the shares of a Dean Witter-sponsored fund only through a Dean Witter broker. Owning shares of an in-house fund may create a bottleneck if you decide to move your account to a different brokerage firm.

Some sales organizations pay their salespeople higher commissions to sell in-house funds compared to the commissions they pay to sell funds from other sponsors. Critics argue that the commission differential can work to an investor's disadvantage because the salesperson has a financial incentive to pitch the firm's products even though an outside sponsor may offer a fund that better fits a customer's needs.

Direct Distribution

Many mutual funds have decided to sell their shares directly to the public, thereby avoiding the need either to employ a sales force or to use outside sales organizations. Direct distributors rely heavily on print advertising to attract investors, as a quick inspection of nearly any issue of *The Wall Street Journal*, *Barron's*, or many other financial publications will attest. Direct distributors have toll-free tele-

> Don't try to time the market. Even professional investors find it difficult (critics say impossible) to regularly forecast market tops and bottoms with any degree of accuracy.

phone numbers and large sales staffs to answer questions and take orders. These firms normally refrain from providing detailed investment advice such as you might expect to receive from a salesperson who is earning a commission. At the same time, many of the sales representatives you reach by telephone will be knowledgeable concerning the funds they sell, including which funds are most suitable to meet a particular investment objective A few mutual fund sponsors that sell direct now offer limited investment advice, a topic that is discussed in Chapter 7.

Mutual funds that choose to sell their shares directly cannot normally be purchased through outside sales organizations because the funds offer salespeople no financial incentives. To buy shares from a fund that sells direct, you must call or write the fund and request an application and a prospectus. These funds generally charge only a small fee, or no fee at all, to buy or redeem their shares. A limited number of discount brokerage companies will purchase shares of certain mutual funds for your brokerage account. This arrangement has certain advantages with regard to record keeping and an ability to use shares to collateralize loans.

Distribution Fees You May Have to Pay

If you feel you need counsel concerning what type of mutual fund to buy or if you have decided to invest in a mutual fund that distributes its shares through a sales force, you are likely to be charged some type of fee by the organization that sells the fund. The fee may be assessed when you purchase shares, or it may be deferred until you present the shares for redemption. Some distributors levy a conditional deferred sales charge that declines the longer you hold the shares. A sub-

Figure 16

MUTUAL FUND FEES AS LISTED IN THE PROSPECTUS

This table is designed to help you understand costs of investing in the fund. These are historical expenses; your actual expenses may be more or less than those shown.

Shareholder Transaction Expenses	
Maximum sales charge on purchases (as a percentage of offering price)	5.75%
Maximum sales charge on reinvested dividends (as a percentage of offering price)	none
Deferred sales charge (as a percentage of original purchase price or redemption proceeds)	none
Redemption fees (as a percentage of amount redeemed)	none
Exchange fee	none
Annual Fund Operating Expenses (for the fiscal year ended September 30, 1991, as a percentage of average net assets)	
Management fees	0.50%
12b-1 expenses	0.17%
Other expenses (audit, legal, shareholder services, transfer agent and custodian)	0.19%
Total fund operating expenses	0.86%

Example	**1 year**	**3 years**	**5 years**	**10 years**
You would pay the following total expenses on a $1,000 investment, assuming 5% annual return[5] and redemption at end of time period.	$66	$83	$102	$157

stantial number of mutual funds also levy a distribution fee that is periodically assessed against the fund's assets. Some fund sponsors even allow you to choose among two or three different fee schedules for the same mutual fund.

A mutual fund's fees are clearly and concisely presented in the prospectus that the fund is required to provide to potential investors. All mutual fund prospectuses present the funds' charges to shareholders in a virtually identical manner, making it relatively easy to compare the fees charged by various funds. A prospectus divides fees into two sections: (1) transaction expenses charged only once during the time a shareholder owns shares in the fund, and (2) annual operating expenses that are charged against the fund's income each year. Fee tables sometimes include all categories of potential fees even though a particular fund may not levy some of the fees. For example, the fee table illustrated in Figure 16 includes an entry for "deferred sales charge" even though this particular fund does not charge such a fee. This prospectus lists "none" when one of the listed fees is not charged by the fund.

Front-End Load Charges

Until the early 1970s the majority of mutual funds were sold by sales agents who were compensated with a sales charge, also called a *load*, equal to 8.5 percent of the amount a customer invested. If you invested $5,000 in one of these funds, a front-end load of $425 (8.5 percent of your $5,000 investment) was immediately deducted to compensate the salesperson and distributor. After deduction of the distribution fee, only $4,575 of the original investment was available to buy shares of the fund. The 8.5 percent sales fee actually amounted to 9.3 percent of the money that went to purchase shares in the fund ($425/$4,575). On the positive side, the era of 8.5 percent loads did not include additional charges for share redemptions.

Money market funds without a sales fee were first offered to investors in the early 1970s. The spectacular success of these funds, combined with an exodus of individuals from the securities markets in general and mutual funds in particular, convinced a number of mutual fund sponsors to bypass their regular sales channels, drop the sales charges, and sell their funds directly to investors. Mutual funds sold without a sales fee are called *no-load funds*. Actually, no-load funds were around for many years prior to the 1970s, but not on a major scale.

The success of mutual fund sponsors that switched to directly distributing their shares, along with the entry of new funds that offered to sell shares directly to investors, helped initiate several important changes in the industry. To compete with the no-loads, some mutual fund sponsors dropped their sales fees and instead charged a redemption fee. These funds merely moved the charge from the opening transaction to the closing transaction, partly so that salespeople could tell potential customers there was no sales charge. "Every dollar you invest will be used to buy shares in the fund," they would note, while glossing over the "redemption surprise." Other funds reduced the size of their sales fee in order to compete with funds sold directly to investors.

Competition among an exploding number of mutual funds has caused a general reduction in the percentage sales fees most funds charge. Although some equity funds con-

> Money market funds that offer unusually high yields may have a large proportion of their portfolio in unsecured corporation short-term debt and a small proportion of their portfolio in lower-yielding U.S. government–guaranteed securities.

tinue to charge an 8.5 percent sales fee, most stock funds sold through brokers, insurance agents, and financial planners charge fees that range from 4 to 6.5 percent of the amount invested. Bond funds sold through sales organizations generally have sales fees of 3 to 5 percent of the amount invested.

Many mutual fund sponsors that levy a front-end sales fee reduce the fee for large purchases. For example, a fund might charge a 6 percent sales fee for an investor's purchases up to $10,000, 5 percent on purchases of $10,001 to $25,000, 4 percent on purchases of $25,001 to $50,000, and so forth. Both the fees and the amounts that must be invested to gain a reduction in the fees vary from fund to fund.

In an unusual twist, the renewed popularity of mutual funds during the 1980s bull market in both stocks and bonds caused some no-load funds to begin charging sales fees, not to pay a salesperson but to provide the mutual funds with an additional source of revenue that was used to attract new investors. The fees initiated by the former no-loads were generally small, often 3 percent or less, thereby earning a new fee classification, *low-load funds.*

Among the funds that charge a load, fees tend to be higher for equity funds than for bond funds, and among stock funds, fees are generally higher for specialized funds that have a relatively small market and are likely to be difficult for a salesperson to explain to potential investors. Many specialized funds are subject to substantial price volatility that attracts investors who are more interested in performance than in saving 1 or 2 percent in sales fees.

Some funds that have a front-end load also charge a sales fee on reinvested dividends and capital gains distributions. This expense applies only if you have elected to reinvest your distributions in additional shares of a fund's stock. Fortunately, funds that levy this fee are the exception rather than the rule.

Redemption Fees

Redemption fees (also called *back-end loads*) are paid when shares are redeemed rather than when shares are purchased. Many mutual fund sponsors have substituted redemption fees for front-end loads because they believe the deferred fees are more palatable to investors, thus making the funds easier to sell. The swelling federal deficit and mountain of personal debt serve as monuments to the willingness of the American people to put off the pain of paying for anything.

Some funds, including many sponsored by brokerage companies, levy a *conditional deferred sales charge* based on the length of time you have held the shares being redeemed. For example, a fund might charge a 6 percent fee when shares have been held less than a year, 5 percent when shares have been held more than one year but less than two years, 4 percent when shares have been held more than two years but less than three, and so forth. Using this particular fee schedule, you would escape a deferred sales charge if you held shares six years or more. A contingent deferred sales charge guarantees a minimum return to the sponsor either from annual expense charges (if you stay in the fund) or the deferred sales charge (if you hold the shares for less than six years). The contingent fee is appealing to investors who are offered an opportunity to purchase mutual fund shares without paying any sales fees. A contingent deferred sales charge may be calculated on the basis of the amount you have invested or the value of your shares.

Figure 17

EFFECT OF FRONT-END LOAD VS. DEFERRED SALES CHARGE ON AN INVESTMENT IN A MUTUAL FUND

	Fund with Front-End Load	Fund with Deferred Sales Charge
Amount invested	$10,000	$10,000
Front-end load (4%)	400	0
Net investment	$ 9,600	$10,000
Value of net investment in 10 years assuming 7% average annual growth	$18,885	$19,672
Deferred sales charge (4%)*	0	787
Net proceeds	$18,885	$18,885

*Assumes deferred sales charge is based on redemption value rather than purchase price. Also assumes the deferred charge is not reduced according to the length of the holding period.

Does it really make any difference whether you are charged a 4 percent front-end load or a 4 percent redemption fee? Suppose you invest $10,000 in a front-end load fund that annually increases in value by 7 percent for ten years, at which time you redeem your shares. Figure 17 illustrates that your $9,600 net investment ($10,000 less the $400 initial sales charge) will increase in ten years to $18,885 if the fund averages a 7 percent annual return. Now suppose the fund charges a 4 percent redemption fee on the proceeds rather than a 4 percent front-end load. Your $10,000 investment will amount to $19,672 at the end of ten years, but you will be required to pay a deferred sales fee equal to 4 percent of the terminal value, or $787, leaving $18,885, the same amount calculated with the 4 percent front-end load. This example assumes that the deferred sales charge is calculated on the value of the shares that are redeemed. If the redemption fee had been based on the price at which the shares were purchased, the comparison would favor the redemption fee over the front-end load assuming the fund earns a positive return.

Annual Fees to Cover Selling Expenses

Some mutual funds cover all or a portion of their sales and marketing expenses, sometimes including payments to salespeople, by charging a monthly fee calculated as a percentage of the average daily assets being managed. For example, a fund may establish an annual charge equal to .5 percent of the fund's average daily assets. The charge, called a *12b-1 fee* after the 1980 SEC rule that permits investment companies to assess the fee, is sometimes used in place of a front-end load or a deferred sales charge, or it may be charged *in addition to* one or both of these other fees. The 12b-1 fee is typically quite small and cannot annually exceed 1.25 percent, but the recurring charge causes a long-term investor to incur substantial costs over the course of many years. The

> Avoid purchasing shares of a closed-end investment company as part of a new issue. These shares will generally decline in price immediately following their issue.

SEC's intent in allowing a 12b-1 fee was to provide mutual funds with the financial resources to attract new investors, thus increasing the amount of assets managed by the funds. The growth in assets, in turn, would permit the funds to achieve economies of scale and reduce their expense ratios.

Annual fees used to pay for mutual fund marketing expenses were initially called *hidden loads* because the charges were buried among other annual expenses. Thus, a mutual fund could trim its front-end or back-end load and initiate a 12b-1 fee to more effectively compete for the money of investors who sought to avoid sales and redemption fees. In reality, a relatively modest annual fee can prove more expensive to an investor than either a front-end load or a redemption fee.

A 1 percent annual 12b-1 fee reduces your return by 1 percent for each year you own the mutual fund. The continuing expense eventually can cause this fee to be more costly than either a front-end load or a back-end load if you own a mutual fund for many years. Figure 18 compares the effects of a 1 percent annual 12b-1 fee and a 6 percent one-time front-end load on a $10,000 investment over a period of fifteen years. The chart assumes an annual return of 13 percent (reduced to 12 percent for the 12b-1 fund). An investment in the fund with the 6 percent load is initially worth less than the same investment in the 12b-1 fund, but at the end of seven years the fund with the front-end load is worth $22,114 while the 12b-1 fund has a value of $22,107. The gap continues to widen in subsequent years as the 1 percent annual fee eats away at the 12b-1 fund's value.

Some sponsors allow investors to choose between two fee structures for the same fund. The choice is generally between either a front-end load or a recurring fee plus a con-

Figure 18

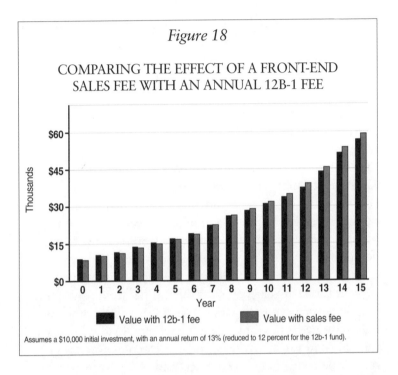

COMPARING THE EFFECT OF A FRONT-END SALES FEE WITH AN ANNUAL 12B-1 FEE

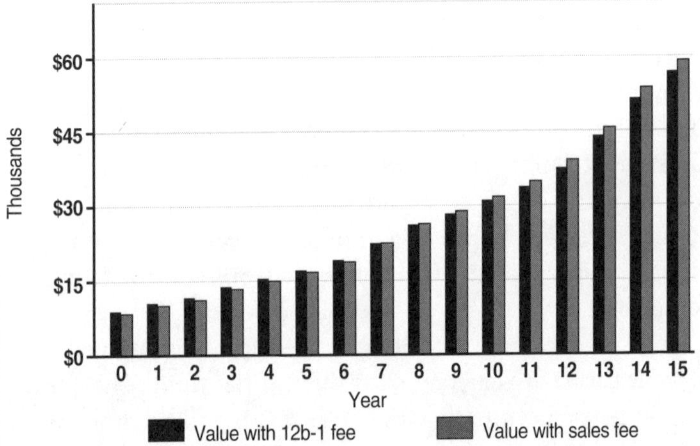

Assumes a $10,000 initial investment, with an annual return of 13% (reduced to 12 percent for the 12b-1 fund).

tingent deferred sales charge. For example, one large mutual fund offers investors a choice of buying Class A shares and paying a maximum 6.5 percent front-end load (reduced for purchases exceeding $10,000) or of buying Class B shares and paying an annual 1 percent 12b-1 fee along with a contingent deferred sales charge of up to 4 percent. The Class B shares have no front-end sales charge. The contingent sales charge, based on the original cost of the shares, is reduced by 1 percent for each year the fund is held. If you planned to hold the shares for an extended period, you would be better served by selecting the Class A shares.

Figure 19

FEES CHARGED BY SELECTED MUTUAL FUNDS

Fund	Sales Charge (%)	Expense Ratio (%)
Equity funds		
Dreyfus Third Century	0	1.17
Fidelity Magellan	3.00	0.96
Keystone America Omega	5.75	1.41
Lexington Goldfund	0	1.63
New England Value	5.75	1.41
T. Rowe Price New Horizons	0	0.93
Putnam Health Sciences	5.75	1.12
Scudder Global	0	1.45
Value Line	0	0.85
Vanguard Index 500	0	0.19
Bond funds		
Dean Witter High-Yield Securities	5.50	0.69
Dreyfus GNMA	0	0.97
Fidelity Government Securities	0	0.72
Kemper Municipal Bond	4.50	0.65
Merrill Lynch Intermediate Term	1.00	0.92
Nuveen Municipal Bond	4.50	0.84
Scudder California Tax-Free	0	0.97
Strong Short-Term Bond	0	0.96
Twentieth Century U.S. Government	0	0.70
Value Line U.S. Government Securities	0	0.67

Consider a single-state money market fund or municipal bond fund if you reside in a state with a high tax rate.

Evaluating Distribution Fees

Distribution fees should be an important consideration when you choose a mutual fund. If you have a relatively good understanding of your own investment needs, how mutual funds operate, the importance of funds' investment objectives, and what type of investment objectives best meets your needs, you may want to select among mutual funds with no front- or back-end loads and no 12b-1 fees. On the other hand, if you are unsure not only about what particular fund to invest in, but what type of fund to buy, a reasonable distribution charge may be money well spent if the person selling the fund can provide you with worthwhile investment advice. Keep in mind that a larger fee does not necessarily mean you will receive better advice.

Be certain to examine a mutual fund's expense ratio at the same time you evaluate distribution costs. A fund may keep its distribution fees low but impose relatively high annual charges to cover operating expenses. Some studies indicate that a mutual fund with a reasonable front-end load can actually produce better results than no-load funds over long periods of time because load funds tend to have smaller expense ratios. This is a generalization, of course, and it is important that you consider all the costs of investing in a particular fund. Fortunately, the mutual fund prospectus makes this task relatively easy.

CHAPTER 7

Selecting a Mutual Fund

Before committing your money to a mutual fund, you should first determine what you expect from your investments. Defining your own financial goals will assist you in selecting mutual funds with investment objectives that are compatible with your needs. The diversification and professional management provided by a mutual fund do not eliminate the risk of investing. The prospectus provided by a mutual fund is one of the best sources of information about the fees, investment objectives, and past performance of the fund.

With over 6,000 mutual funds ready and willing to take your money, it is difficult to determine where you should invest. Should you choose a fund that sells its shares directly to investors, thereby saving a sales or redemption fee? Should you trust your broker and invest in the mutual funds he or she recommends even though you will have to pay a sales or redemption charge? Should you buy into a fund based mostly on last year's investment performance, or should you be concerned more about a fund's long-term performance? How important is a mutual fund's expense ratio? Should you search for a fund with a relatively stable net asset value, or do you have to accept price variation in order to have a chance to earn substantial capital gains? You should consider many factors in selecting a mutual fund.

Sorting Out Your Investment Goals

Unless you are unusually wealthy, you will never be able to acquire everything that you desire: exotic vacations, new automobiles every two or three years, jewelry, early retirement, sending the kids to private school and then on to a "name" college. The list is limited only by your imagination. Unfortunately, limited financial resources are likely to keep you from achieving many of your goals, including some goals you consider quite important. Unless you establish a system to prioritize your goals, you will spend your limited financial resources on many things that you deem fairly unimportant, and you will miss out on some financial goals that you consider crucial.

It may seem farfetched to believe people would spend money on things that are not high on their wish list, but how many people do you know who buy whatever happens to present itself first? They see new clothes and buy them. A new appliance? No problem. Whatever first comes down the pike consumes their income and their savings. Lack of a spending plan causes these individuals to sacrifice their long-term goals simply because they occur later, after all the money has been used up.

This is not the way you lead your own life, of course. You are more thoughtful and deliberative. So how much financial assistance will you be able to provide for your children's college education? When will you be able to afford to retire? How frequently should you be trading automobiles? To get a handle on answers to these and other questions that are important to your financial health, you need to draw up a list of your goals and—this is the difficult part—determine which of these goals are most important to you and your family. The goals you establish and when you want to meet them plays a major part in selecting the mutual funds you will use to achieve your goals.

The process of establishing and evaluating financial goals is important but somewhat afield for an introductory book on mutual funds. The topic of goal setting is addressed in detail in *The Guide to Personal Budgeting*, another book in this series. The short and sweet of it is that you need to estimate the cost and approximate date for each of your major financial goals. The amounts you need to accumulate and the date the funds are required are major determinants of the types of mutual funds you should choose to own.

Matching Mutual Funds with Your Financial Goals

It is important to choose mutual funds with investment objectives that are compatible with your goals. If you are in

> Be sure to consider annual management and operating fees as well as sales fees when you select a fund, especially if you are a long-term investor. Relatively high annual fees can rapidly overtake any one-time savings from buying a no-load fund.

your twenties and interested in an early start on a retirement fund, you will be interested in a mutual fund that emphasizes capital growth rather than current income or liquidity. Electing to go with an equity fund whose investment objective is capital growth eliminates the majority of mutual funds from your consideration. At the opposite end of the investment spectrum, equity funds and long-term bond funds are not appropriate investment tools to serve as an emergency fund where safety, stability, and liquidity are important requirements.

Choosing Funds with Appropriate Investment Horizons

Rather than selecting a separate mutual fund to serve as an investment vehicle for each goal you have identified, you should attempt to realize your goals by pursuing an overall investment strategy. Are your goals heavily weighted toward the long-term (as would be the case for retirement or eventual college financial assistance for young children)? If so, you should concentrate your investments in mutual funds that have long-term investment objectives. On the other hand, if you are mostly concerned about current income, you need to concentrate your investments in mutual funds with portfolios of bonds or income stocks.

Most individuals have a combination of goals that require a blended portfolio of several mutual funds. You are likely to be best served by owning shares in three types of funds: a money market fund, an intermediate- or long-term bond fund, and an equity fund. The money market fund provides stability and liquidity to take care of emergencies and other immediate needs, the bond fund provides current dividends to supplement your other income, and the equity fund provides (hopefully) capital appreciation that will assist you in achieving your long-term goals. It is generally poor investment policy to place all your savings in a single fund or in several funds with a common investment objective.

Whether you choose to invest in an aggressive equity fund or a more conservative equity fund depends primarily on your risk tolerance and your goals. If you consider a goal to be particularly important and you feel that it can be achieved without taking high risks, you should probably settle for a conservative fund that will not exhibit large price swings. On the other hand, if you will only be able to achieve a certain goal by earning a very high rate of return, you may decide on an all-or-nothing investment and choose an aggressive growth fund.

Suppose, in dollar terms, you estimate that your goals are 60 percent long-term, 25 percent intermediate-term, and 15 percent short-term. You should go about establishing a mutual fund portfolio that is compatible with this mix of goals. Another investor who has goals and monetary requirements that are different from your own is likely to need a portfolio of mutual funds that is also different. Long-term personal financial goals are best met with mutual funds that have long-term investment goals while short-term personal financial needs are best met with mutual funds that strive for current income, stability of value, liquidity, and safety of principal.

Figure 20

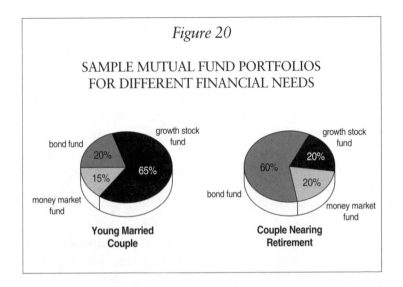

SAMPLE MUTUAL FUND PORTFOLIOS
FOR DIFFERENT FINANCIAL NEEDS

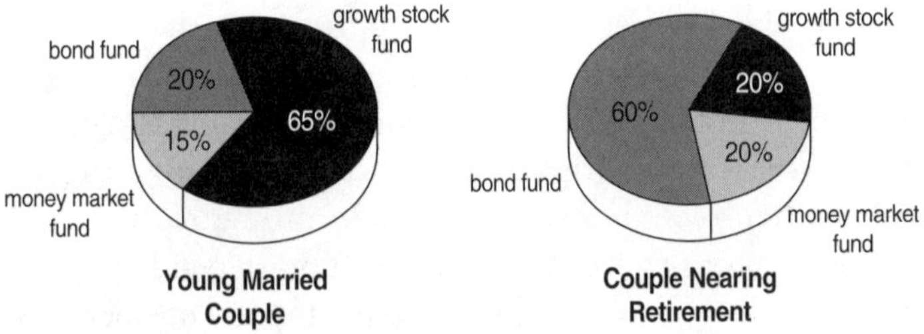

You should constantly reevaluate the goals you establish. As you grow older and are able to achieve certain goals while foregoing others, you are likely to want to revise the goals that remain and to reallocate your existing mutual fund investments. For example, once you successfully establish an emergency fund, you may want to concentrate a larger proportion of your subsequent investments in mutual funds that have long-term investment objectives. Likewise, as you close in on retirement, you should consider moving money out of growth funds and into income funds that provide greater stability of income and value. The mix of your investment portfolio is known as *asset allocation*. Altering the mix of investments is more convenient if you own mutual funds that are part of a family of funds that allows switching of your investment among various funds.

Choosing Funds with Appropriate Risk Characteristics

Mutual funds are not all equally risky. Some funds own securities that have very volatile market prices. A mutual fund that invests in stocks with volatile market prices will have a volatile net asset value because stocks tend to rise and fall in price together. If you invest in a mutual fund that owns volatile stocks and need to sell your shares on short notice, you may realize a large loss in value. Of course, it is also possible that you will sell your shares for a large profit, but the uncertainty of not knowing how much you will receive for your shares makes the shares risky to own. It isn't necessarily wrong to invest in a mutual fund that has a volatile net asset value, of course, if the fund meets your investment needs and you understand the risks.

Mutual funds that invest in long-term government or corporate bonds are subject to major changes in net asset value whenever long-term interest rates change. A large increase in long-term interest rates will cause a substantial decline in the net asset value of a long-term bond fund. You must decide if the higher current return from a long-term bond fund is worth the added volatility of the fund's net asset value. If there is a likelihood you will have to sell your shares on short notice, you should probably consider buying shares in an intermediate-term bond fund rather than a long-term bond fund because intermediate-term bonds do not vary as much in value as long-term bonds.

A major consideration in determining your risk tolerance is the importance you attach to the goals you are attempting to achieve. The more important the goals, the less tolerance you have for risky investments. For example, you may have certain goals you simply cannot take a chance on not achieving. Suppose you are nearing retirement and have been putting aside money to supplement your social security and employer-sponsored pension. If this supplemental income will be critical to your financial well-being, you will want to move your investment funds to a mutual fund that provides high current income but with great safety of principal. You should not trust all of your retirement money to an equity fund or a mutual fund that invests in high-yield, high-risk bonds. Rather, you should choose a fund that invests in high-grade corporate securities or U.S. government securities. In truth, you may want to hedge your bets and invest in two funds with similar investment objectives.

If there is some possibility that your living expenses will require all of your investment income and a portion of your investment principal (i.e., require you to periodically sell some of your mutual fund shares), the stability of the net asset value of your shares becomes an important consideration. The problem you face is that mutual funds with stable NAVs typically provide fairly modest returns. A solution may be to keep a portion of your savings in a money market fund or a short-term bond fund at the same time that you maintain a position in one or more income funds.

Buying Directly vs. Buying from a Salesperson

The previous chapter discussed the differences between buying mutual funds directly and buying mutual funds through a broker, insurance agent, or financial planner. Buying funds directly will reduce or eliminate sales and redemption fees, although you must generally give up the advice to which you are entitled when you buy shares through a broker or financial planner. If you know so little about investing that you have no idea what *type* of mutual fund (aggressive growth fund, bond fund, or money market fund) to buy, you should probably bite the bullet and buy shares from a salesperson who can assist you with investment advice. If you choose this option, you should keep in mind that the salesperson has a vested interest in making his or her investment product look as good as possible.

You are more than half way home if you have sorted through your financial goals and understand your financial situation well enough so that you feel comfortable determining the types of mutual funds you should buy. A number of information sources can assist you in selecting individual funds within categories. A select group of these sources is discussed in Chapter 9. Some sources provide substantial detail including historical returns, expenses, and ratings. Of course, if you rely on these publications to assist you in selecting mutual funds, you will have to spend time conducting your own research. Time and effort are the prices you must pay for going it alone.

Free or low-cost investment advice has recently opened up for mutual fund investors. A few mutual funds that sell direct are now offering limited investment advice. In 1991, Dreyfus Corporation started giving free asset-allocation advice to individual investors. The company provides a recommended mix of bonds, stocks, and money-market investments based on financial information supplied on a Dreyfus questionnaire by individual investors. In late 1992, Fidelity Investments announced a new program that offered to recommend a mix of Fidelity mutual funds to best meet an individual's particular needs. The recommendation is

You should generally avoid buying shares in a mutual fund that concentrates its investments in a single industry. These *sector funds* are risky investments that don't serve the interests of most individual investors.

based on information you supply on a Fidelity questionnaire. Fidelity also operates an advisory service that offers to manage individual portfolios of mutual funds for a maximum fee of 1 percent of annual assets. The service requires a minimum portfolio of $100,000.

Selecting Funds on the Basis of Past Performance

Investors who feel comfortable selecting mutual funds without the aid of a salesperson are likely to be influenced by the funds' historical investment performance. Even investors who follow the recommendation of an investment advisor are usually swayed by the returns a fund has earned for its shareholders. Americans may have a proud history of rooting for the underdog, but most mutual fund investors prefer to put their money in funds that have a record of superior investment performance. So is past performance any guide to future performance? Should you select a mutual fund based primarily on the fund's historical returns?

Evaluating mutual funds on the basis of the returns they have earned for investors in years past requires an adjustment of the returns for risk. Financial theorists believe that taking greater risks tends to produce greater returns over a long period of time. Thus, mutual funds such as aggressive growth funds or junk bond funds that own securities that entail substantial risk will, over time, provide investors with superior investment returns. Common stock funds should earn higher returns than corporate bond funds, and corporate bond funds should earn higher returns than government bond funds. These relationships do not hold true every month or every year or even over every period of several years. Over the long haul, however, the evidence supports the linkage between risk and return.

Hundreds of tests evaluating mutual fund performance have been undertaken, and the majority of these tests indicate the following:

1. Mutual fund managements have difficulty earning a risk-adjusted return that is superior to the return that can be earned from a naive buy-and-hold strategy.
2. Sales and redemption charges and expense ratios are important in explaining the differences in risk-adjusted returns among mutual funds. This indicates you should make your choices among funds that have low expenses and modest or no sales and redemption charges.
3. Short-term investment performance is not a good indicator of how a mutual fund will perform in future periods. Don't select a mutual fund based on the fund's return during the past six months or the past year.
4. If a mutual fund's historical returns over a longer period of time are going to be an important decision criterion, make certain to find out if the fund's management has recently changed. Good management can quickly turn into mediocre management when the superior talent goes elsewhere.
5. Mutual fund managements tend to have difficulty timing the market. That is, professional portfolio managers are generally unable to forecast overall market movements or movements in particular sectors on any kind of con-

sistent basis. This means you should beware of buying mutual funds that have unusually large portfolio turnovers. Extensive trading is likely to increase costs and decrease investor returns.

The Advantages of Dollar-Cost Averaging

Although not a technique for selecting mutual funds, dollar-cost averaging is a worthwhile investment technique. Dollar-cost averaging is nothing new, and the methodology is easy to understand and implement.

If professional portfolio managers have difficulty choosing the best time to invest, there is no reason to believe that individual investors can do any better. Many financial advisors suggest that individuals are best served by investing a constant amount of money at regular intervals, a technique termed *dollar-cost averaging*. Dollar-cost averaging requires that you invest equal amounts of money each month or each quarter regardless of how the market performs and regardless of what you expect the market to do in future months. Rather than attempt to outguess the market and invest only when you forecast rising stock prices or rising bond prices, you forge ahead and build your mutual fund portfolio period by period without regard to near-term price movements.

One mistake individual investors often make is to get cold feet and quit investing (or sell existing investments) during the later stages of a major decline in security prices. Thus, individual investors often leave the market when stock prices are relatively low and a moderate investment could purchase a relatively large number of mutual fund shares. Using dollar-cost averaging, a constant dollar investment buys a larger number of shares when a mutual fund's shares have declined in value. The lower the offering price of a mutual fund's shares, the more shares you are able to purchase each period. A rising market causes you to purchase fewer shares each period with the same dollar investment.

Figure 21 illustrates the investment record for a person who has implemented a dollar-cost averaging investment program over a four-year period. During the first two years, the individual invested $500 per quarter in the shares of a mutual fund. This investment is increased to $600 per quarter in the following two years. The investor is able to purchase 46.512 shares of the mutual fund in the first quarter when the offering price is $10.75. In the last quarter of 1997, when the offering price has risen to $12.50, $500 buys only 40 shares of the fund. The far right column shows the average price paid for all the shares held at any time.

An investment program of dollar-cost averaging does not dictate that you always maintain exactly the same periodic investment. If your income increases you can occasionally increase the amount of your monthly or quarterly investment. You should never alter the amount of your investment because of a change in your assessment of the market. Dollar-cost averaging takes out of your hands the decision of how much and when to invest at the same time it requires the discipline to continue investing in the face of an occasionally discouraging market.

> Novice investors should generally stick with funds that have proven management and a good long-term track record.

Figure 21

EXAMPLE OF DOLLAR-COST AVERAGING

Year	Quarter	Amount Invested	Purchase Price/Sh	Shares Purchased	Shares Owned	Average Price
1996	I	$500	$10.75	46.512	46.512	$10.75
	II	500	11.25	44.444	90.956	10.99
	III	500	12.00	41.667	132.623	11.31
	IV	500	11.00	45.455	178.078	11.23
1997	I	500	11.50	43.478	221.556	11.28
	II	500	11.75	42.553	264.109	11.36
	III	500	12.25	40.816	304.925	11.48
	IV	500	12.50	40.000	344.925	11.60
1998	I	600	12.75	47.059	391.984	11.74
	II	600	13.00	46.154	438.138	11.87
	III	600	12.75	47.059	485.197	11.95
	IV	600	13.00	46.154	531.351	12.04
1999	I	600	13.50	44.444	575.795	12.15
	II	600	13.25	45.283	621.078	12.24
	III	600	12.75	47.059	668.137	12.27
	IV	600	13.00	46.154	714.291	12.32

Total amount invested	$8,800
Portfolio value after four years	$9,864

Dollar-cost averaging can be applied to simultaneous investments in different mutual funds. Suppose you determine that you will invest $1,000 each quarter. Depending upon your goals and financial circumstances, you might decide on a quarterly investment of $600 in a stock growth fund, $250 in an intermediate-term bond fund, and $150 in a

> Beware of purchasing an investment trust that sells for more than the underlying principal value of the assets owned by the trust. Trust units that sell at a premium price will gradually (or rapidly) lose value as bonds in the trust are redeemed at par.

money market fund. Changing the allocation of your investments among these funds would be compatible with dollar-cost averaging so long as you made changes in response to changes in your financial needs rather than to changes in the market.

Importance of the Prospectus

The first order of business when you consider an investment in a mutual fund is to obtain a copy of the fund's prospectus. The second order of business is to study the document you have just acquired. If you have a good idea of the type of fund (i.e., a fund with an appropriate investment objective) you want to own but you are unsure about which particular fund to purchase, obtain prospectuses for several funds. Mutual funds do not charge for these documents. Never, never, never buy the shares of a mutual fund without first reading the fund's prospectus. A mutual fund or an agent of the fund is required to supply you with a prospectus that fully describes the fund's objectives, management, and fees. Although funds are permitted to accept a purchase order and send the prospectus along with a purchase confirmation, you should request the prospectus prior to placing an order. A prospectus can be obtained directly from a fund (for funds that distribute shares directly) or from an agent of the fund (for funds that distribute shares through a sales force). In March of 1993, the Securities and Exchange Commission unveiled a proposal that would allow mutual funds to sell shares through the mail without first offering a propectus.

When you receive the prospectus, *read it!* Even though the document contains legal jargon that is sometimes difficult to interpret, there is enough valuable and understandable information in a prospectus to make it worth your time to carefully review this important document before you invest your money. A prospectus bares a mutual fund's soul to anyone who is interested enough to take a peek. In particular you should look for these points:

1. The fund's investment objective. Is the fund's goal to maximize dividend income, maximize interest income, earn short-term gains, seek long-term capital growth, provide a stable share price, or earn tax-exempt income? Will the fund meet its stated objective by investing in short-term municipal securities, common stocks, long-term corporate bonds, or intermediate-term government bonds? Does the fund's management plan cause it to engage in frequent trading? A mutual fund's investment objective is a major determinant of the types of securities held in the fund's portfolio and of the risks you will face as a shareholder of the fund. It is very important that you select a fund whose investment goal is compatible with your own financial objectives.
2. The fees charged and the impact of these fees on your investment in the fund. Because mutual funds can levy several different types of fees, it is important that you understand the charges you will pay if you purchase shares in the fund. Not all mutual funds charge the same

Figure 22

FINANCIAL STATEMENT FROM
A MUTUAL FUND PROSPECTUS

Condensed Financial Information

The information in the following table has been audited by Ernst & Young, the Fund's independent auditors, whose report thereon appears in the Fund's Statement of Additional Information. Further financial data and related notes are included in the Fund's Statement of Additional Information, available upon request.

Per Share Income and Capital Changes

Selected data for a share of partnership interest outstanding throughout each year.

	Year Ended December 31,				
	1987[1]	1988	1989	1990	1991
Per Share Data:					
Investment income	$ .34	$ 1.62	$ 4.20	$ 5.63	$ 4.27
Operating expenses[2]	.17	.32	1.41	1.99	2.09
Interest expense, loan commitment fees and dividends on securities sold short	.09	.14	1.47	1.27	.11
Total expenses[2]	.26	.46	2.88	3.26	2.20
Investment income—net	.08	1.16	1.32	2.37	2.07
Net realized and unrealized gain (loss) on investments	9.38	.09[4]	2.34	(4.47)	6.85
Net increase (decrease) in net asset value resulting from operations	9.46	1.25	3.66	(2.10)	8.92
Net asset value:					
Beginning of year	15.00	24.46	25.71	29.37	27.27
End of year	$24.46	$25.71	$29.37	$27.27	$36.19
Ratios To Average Net Assets:					
Investment income	3.10%[3]	7.00%	4.47%	4.25%	3.06%
Operating expenses[2]	1.57[3]	1.39	1.50	1.50	1.50
Interest expense, loan commitment fees and dividends on securities sold short	.81[3]	.59	1.56	.96	.08
Total expenses[2]	2.38[3]	1.98	3.06	2.46	1.58
Investment income–net	.72[3]	5.02	1.41	1.79	1.48
Net realized and unrealized gain (loss) on investments	7.60[3]	(2.18)	12.29	(11.00)	27.48
Net increase (decrease) in net assets resulting from operations	8.32%[3]	2.84%	13.70%	(9.21%)	28.96%
Portfolio Turnover Rate	431.64%[3]	831.14%	370.97%	188.16%	95.49%
Thousands of Shares Outstanding at End of Year	3,800	6,151	3,721	2,215	1,687

(1)From March 27, 1987 (commencement of operations) to December 31, 1987.
(2)Net of expenses reimbursed.
(3)Not annualized.
(4)In addition to the net realized and unrealized loss on investments, this amount includes an increase in net asset value per share resulting from the timing of issuances and redemptions of Fund shares in relation to fluctuating market values for the portfolio.

types of fees or the same level of fees. The fund's fees and the effect of these fees are described in the first part of the prospectus.

3. How to purchase and redeem shares of the fund. A section of Chapter 6 described several methods used by mutual funds to distribute their shares to investors. The prospectus will explain if the fund allows you to buy shares directly or whether you must go through an outside salesperson. It will also describe how the fund's shares can be redeemed.

> Don't acquire shares in so many different funds that you have difficulty keeping track of what you own. Few individuals need to own shares in more than four or five funds.

4. A financial statement illustrating the per-share income and capital changes during the ten previous years. The historical financial statement provides a look at the fund's past investment performance, thus allowing you to compare the performance of one fund with the performance of competing funds. The financial statement details annual income, expenses, investment income, dividends, gains on investments, and changes in net asset value.
5. The services offered and how these services operate. The prospectus will explain whether the fund's sponsor offers features such as dividend reinvestment, check writing, and tax-sheltered retirement plans. Even though numerous funds may offer the same basic services, the fees they charge for these services may vary enough to influence your preference. For example, some funds charge a nominal fee for each check you write or for each switch of your money from one fund to another from the same sponsor. Likewise, some mutual fund sponsors are more lenient about allowing transfers from one fund to another. These differences may affect your decision to purchase shares of the fund.

CHAPTER 8

Mutual Fund Alternatives: Closed-End Funds and Unit Investment Trusts

Mutual funds are not the only type of investment that offers immediate diversification and professional selection of securities for individuals who have modest amounts of money to invest. Closed-end investment companies invest in a portfolio of securities with capital raised from selling a limited number of shares. These investment companies do not stand ready to redeem their shares on demand. Another type of investment, the unit investment trust, maintains the same portfolio of securities and does not require active portfolio management. These alternatives each offer advantages and disadvantages when compared to mutual funds.

Mutual funds offer diversification and professional management of securities portfolios—two desirable investment attributes that most individual investors have difficulty providing for themselves. Mutual funds also have a down side. For one thing, the funds charge ongoing operating and management fees that reduce the returns you earn as a shareholder. These charges are not necessarily unfair because there are unavoidable costs associated with managing a large investment portfolio. On the other hand, management fees charged by some large funds produce revenues that far exceed the costs of operating these funds. Many mutual funds also levy sales or redemption charges that must be paid by shareholders.

A mutual fund's unique organizational structure can cause shareholders to suffer financial penalties. Mutual funds continually accept new investors and redeem the shares of existing investors so that mutual fund portfolio managers must adjust their investment policies to account for monies that flow into and out of the funds. Successful funds sometimes sell so many new shares and grow so rapidly that the portfolio managers have a difficult time identifying appropriate uses for the monies.

Closed-End Investment Companies

Closed-end investment companies are operated in much the same manner as mutual funds. These companies employ professional portfolio managers who assemble and oversee portfolios of securities for the benefit of the firms' shareholders. The companies distribute dividend and interest income to shareholders, who are required to pay taxes on the distributions. Closed-end investment companies also distribute capital gains realized from the sale of securities that have increased in value. These funds levy an ongoing charge to pay for the costs of operating the fund and managing the fund's portfolio. So far, the description of a closed-end investment company makes it seem identical to the mutual funds discussed throughout this book.

The Organization of Closed-End Investment Companies

The major difference between closed-end investment companies and mutual funds is the limited number of shares issued by closed-end funds. These firms raise capital by issuing a limited number of shares at the time they are organized. Additional shares of a closed-end fund are not continuously offered for sale and, in fact, are unlikely ever to be offered. Likewise, closed-end funds do not stand ready to redeem outstanding shares whenever shareholders decide that they would like to dispose of their investment. Closed-end investment companies are organized in an identical manner to all other corporations that have publicly traded common stock. The company initially issues a limited number of shares and may later sell additional shares, but only with the approval of the firm's existing shareholders. Closed-end investment company shares that are distributed as part of a new issue are expected by the fund's manage-

> Understand that investing in global and foreign stock funds can subject you to losses in the event that the dollar strengthens against foreign currencies.

ment and by investors to remain outstanding indefinitely (i.e., no redemptions will occur).

Suppose a sponsor forms a new closed-end investment company that has an investment objective of earning high current income for its shareholders. The fund's portfolio managers intend to accomplish the objective by investing shareholders' money in medium-quality, long-term corporate bonds. The fund's sponsor employs the services of an investment banking firm that solicits investors to buy 20 million shares of the fund's stock at a price of $10 per share. The portfolio manager will have somewhat less than $200 million to invest because a portion of the money raised from investors must be shared with the investment banking firm. For example, the investment banker may retain 30 cents per share distributed, causing the investment company to receive $9.70 for each share issued.

The types of bonds held in the fund's portfolio will determine the amount of interest income the fund will earn and the amount of dividends the fund's shareholders will receive. If interest rates happen to be relatively high when the fund is organized, the portfolio manager will assemble a portfolio of high-coupon bonds that will earn high interest income for the fund and enable the fund to pay hefty dividends to its shareholders. If interest rates are relatively low when the fund is formed, dividend payments to shareholders will be more modest. So long as the closed-end fund continues to hold the same bonds, the fund's interest income and dividend distributions to the fund's shareholders will remain the same. Only if some of the fund's bonds are redeemed by their issuers or if the managers trade bonds held in the fund's portfolio will shareholder dividends change.

If market rates of interest subsequently decline following

formation of the fund, there will be an increase in the market values of all fixed-income securities including bonds held in the fund's portfolio. In fact, because this fund's sponsors have decided to concentrate on owning bonds with long maturities, the fund's portfolio will gain substantially in value because of reduced interest rates. An increased portfolio value, in turn, is likely to cause an increase in the value of each of the fund's outstanding shares.

Because no additional shares of stock are being issued by the fund, the portfolio managers will not have to be concerned about investing a large inflow of new money in low-coupon bonds (remember, interest rates have fallen) that would cause a reduction in the dividends paid to each of the fund's original shareholders. Likewise, the fund's portfolio managers will not have to be concerned about selling bonds from the portfolio to pay off shareholders who decide to redeem their shares of the fund. Closed-end investment companies do not offer to redeem shares of their own stock.

Closed-end investment companies are managed as ongoing firms that pay portfolio managers to continually evaluate and adjust the funds' securities portfolios. The proceeds from the sale of stocks or bonds from a fund's portfolio are reinvested in other stocks or bonds that are considered more promising investments. For example, managers of an equity growth fund who expect a substantial decline in the stock market are likely to sell some of the fund's stocks or move a portion of the fund's portfolio to more conservative stocks. Managers of a bond fund who are expecting market rates of interest to increase are likely to decrease the average maturity length of the fund's bond portfolio in order to reduce losses that will occur in the value of the bonds owned.

How Closed-End Investment Company Shares Are Valued

Closed-end investment company shares are actually accorded two values. Net asset value, the accounting value of an investment company's shares, is calculated in the same manner used to determine the NAV of a mutual fund's shares; the market value of the fund's portfolio is divided by the fund's outstanding shares of stock. For example, a closed-end investment company that owns $18 million of securities (valued at current market prices) and that has 1.2 million outstanding shares has a net asset value of $18 million/1.2 million shares, or $15 per share. If the value of the fund's portfolio increases to $24 million, the new net asset value will be $24 million/1.2 million shares, or $20 per share.

Closed-end investment company shares are also valued according to the price at which the shares are traded among investors. The market value of a closed-end fund's shares may or may not equal the shares' net asset value. In the example just cited in which the fund's shares have an NAV of $15, the shares may trade among investors in the secondary market at a price of more than $15 or less than $15. A closed-end fund does not stand ready to redeem its own shares at net asset value, so shareholders who wish to sell their stock must locate other investors who are interested in buying the shares. The price agreed to by the two parties is likely to be other than the share's net asset value. Shares of closed-end investment companies are priced in the same

> If you plan to select a mutual fund on the basis of past investment performance, make certain that the same investment managers are still employed by the fund.

manner as other stocks traded on the exchanges and in the over-the-counter market.

Why would the shares of a closed-end investment company sell at a price other than their net asset value? Suppose an investment company's portfolio managers are able to produce superior investment performance (compared to other funds and compared to stock market averages) for several consecutive years. Substantial dividends and capital gains distributions are made, the net asset value and share price rise, and stockholders are pleased with their investment in the fund. The outstanding performance garners substantial publicity, causing many investors to consider moving their money to the care of the fund's managers. These investors cannot buy shares directly from the fund (remember, a closed-end fund has a limit on the number of outstanding shares) and must place orders with brokerage firms that will seek out existing shareholders of the fund who might be interested in selling their shares. The current shareholders know that they have a good investment and will be reluctant to part with their shares unless they receive a premium price. Even the best investments are for sale at some price. Investor demand occasioned by superior investment performance is likely to cause the shares of the closed-end investment company to trade at a price that is higher than the net asset value.

Now consider a closed-end fund that employs portfolio managers who have posted poor investment results for several years running. Investors are likely to shun the fund unless the fund's shares sell at a sufficient discount (as judged by investors) from net asset value. The worse the fund's investment performance, the larger the discount investors are likely to demand in order to buy the shares. Why pay full price to buy into a closed-end fund that is managed by professionals who can't even match the returns on a popular stock average?

How Closed-End Investment Company Shares Are Traded

The shares of a closed-end investment company are traded by specialists on the organized exchanges and by securities dealers in the over-the-counter market. The shares of these funds are bought and sold by dealers and specialists at whatever prices cause a relative balance of supply and demand. A dealer who experiences an excess of demand over supply in the shares of a closed-end investment company (investors are buying more shares from the dealer than they are selling to the dealer) is likely to raise the bid price of the shares in order to attract more sellers and to raise the ask price in order to attract fewer buyers.

If you wish to buy or sell shares of a closed-end fund, you must employ the services of a brokerage company that has access to the markets where the shares are traded. If the shares of a closed-end fund have a primary market on the New York Stock Exchange, a brokerage company is likely to execute an order for the fund's shares on the NYSE.

You can participate in a new offering of closed-end investment company shares by entering an order with the investment banker who is bringing the issue to market or with a broker who will purchase shares in the investment company from the investment banker. New closed-end funds with an investment objective compatible with your investment needs are relatively infrequent, and you are likely to end up buying shares in the secondary market.

Figure 23

FRONT PAGE OF PROSPECTUS FOR A NEW CLOSED-END BOND FUND

SUBJECT TO COMPLETION, DATED JUNE 16, 1992

4,000,000 Shares

The China Fund, Inc.

Common Stock

The Fund is a newly incorporated, non-diversified, closed-end management investment company. The Fund's investment objective is long-term capital appreciation which it seeks to achieve by investing primarily in equity securities (i) of companies for which the principal trading market is in the People's Republic of China ("China"), (ii) of companies for which the principal trading market is outside of China, or constituting direct investments (as defined herein) in companies organized outside of China, that in both cases derive at least 50% of their revenues from goods or services sold or produced, or have at least 50% of their assets, in China and (iii) constituting direct investments in companies organized in China (collectively, "China companies"). It is the policy of the Fund, under normal market conditions, to invest substantially all, but not less than 65%, of its assets in equity securities of China companies. The Fund expects to invest up to 25% of the net proceeds of the offering made hereby in direct investments in China companies, with the balance allocated primarily to investments in listed securities. See "Investment Objective and Policies." There can be no assurance that the Fund's investment objective will be achieved. Investments in China companies involve certain risks and special considerations not typically associated with investments in the United States, such as greater government involvement in the economy, political and legal uncertainties and currency fluctuations. Additionally, the Chinese securities markets are emerging markets characterized by a relatively small number of equity issues and relatively low trading volume, resulting in substantially less liquidity and greater price volatility. See "Risk Factors and Special Considerations." The address of the Fund is 405 Lexington Avenue, New York, New York 10174, and the Fund's telephone number is (212) 808-0500. Investors are advised to read this Prospectus and to retain it for future reference.

Wardley Investment Services (Hong Kong) Limited will act as the Fund's investment manager with respect to the Fund's holdings of listed securities. Wardley Direct Investment Management (Hong Kong) Limited will act as the Fund's investment manager with respect to the Fund's direct investments.

Of the 4,000,000 shares of Common Stock offered hereby, 3,000,000 shares are being offered for sale in the United States by the U.S. Underwriters and 1,000,000 shares of Common Stock are being offered for sale outside the United States by the International Managers in concurrent offerings, subject to transfers between the Underwriters of each of the offerings. See "Underwriting."

Prior to the offerings, there has been no public market for the Fund's Common Stock. See "Risk Factors and Special Considerations." The Common Stock has been approved for listing on the New York Stock Exchange under the trading symbol "CHN," subject to notice of issuance.

THESE SECURITIES HAVE NOT BEEN APPROVED OR DISAPPROVED BY THE SECURITIES AND EXCHANGE COMMISSION OR ANY STATE SECURITIES COMMISSION NOR HAS THE SECURITIES AND EXCHANGE COMMISSION OR ANY STATE SECURITIES COMMISSION PASSED UPON THE ACCURACY OR ADEQUACY OF THIS PROSPECTUS. ANY REPRESENTATION TO THE CONTRARY IS A CRIMINAL OFFENSE.

	Price to Public	Underwriting Discount (1)	Proceeds to Fund (2)
Per share	$15.00	$	$
Total (3)	$60,000,000	$	$

(1) See "Underwriting" for information concerning indemnification of the Underwriters and other information.
(2) Before deducting expenses of the offerings estimated at $, payable by the Fund, which include $225,000 to be paid to the Underwriters in partial reimbursement of their expenses.
(3) The Fund has granted the U.S. Underwriters an option, exercisable within 30 days of the date hereof, to purchase up to 600,000 additional shares of Common Stock, at the Price to Public per share, less the Underwriting Discount, for the purpose of covering over-allotments, if any. If the U.S. Underwriters exercise such option in full, the total Price to Public, Underwriting Discount and Proceeds to the Fund would be $69,000,000, $ and $, respectively. See "Underwriting."

The shares of Common Stock are offered by the U.S. Underwriters when, as and if delivered to and accepted by them, subject to their right to withdraw, cancel or reject orders in whole or in part and subject to certain other conditions. It is expected that delivery of the certificates representing the shares will be made against payment on or about July , 1992, at the office of Oppenheimer & Co., Inc., Oppenheimer Tower, World Financial Center, New York, New York 10281.

Oppenheimer & Co., Inc. **Merrill Lynch & Co.**

The date of this Prospectus is July , 1992.

Information contained herein is subject to completion or amendment. A registration statement relating to these securities has been filed with the Securities and Exchange Commission. These securities may not be sold nor may offers to buy be accepted prior to the time the registration statement becomes effective. This prospectus shall not constitute an offer to sell or the solicitation of an offer to buy nor shall there be any sale of these securities in any State in which such offer, solicitation or sale would be unlawful prior to registration or qualification under the securities laws of any such State.

Because closed-end funds do not stand ready to redeem their shares, shareholders who wish to dispose of shares in these funds must locate other investors who are interested in purchasing the shares. An investor who wishes to sell shares in a closed-end fund must ordinarily employ the services of a brokerage company that will be able to sell the shares in a market where the stock is traded.

You will be required to pay a brokerage commission when you purchase shares of a closed-end investment company through a brokerage company. In fact, you must pay a brokerage fee when you purchase shares in the fund and another brokerage fee to sell the same shares. The size of the brokerage fee depends on the size of the transaction and the commission schedule of the brokerage firm you select to undertake the transaction. Some brokerage firms base their fees primarily on the number of shares in a trade (for example, the charge to buy 500 shares of a $10 stock will be substantially higher than the charge to buy 100 shares of a $50 stock) while other brokerage companies primarily base their commissions on the value of the securities in a customer's trade. You may be able to gain significant commission savings by dealing with a discount brokerage firm, rather than a full-service brokerage firm when you buy and sell shares in closed-end investment companies.

Although you must pay normal brokerage fees to buy and sell shares of a closed-end investment company, there are no sales loads or redemption fees like those that are charged by many mutual funds. A closed-end investment company does not need to employ salespeople because there are no additional shares of the fund to sell following the original public offering.

Unit Investment Trusts

Unit investment trusts (UITs), also called *unit trusts* and *investment trusts*, are another investment vehicle that offers both immediate diversification and professional selection of securities. UITs are particularly popular with investors who seek tax-exempt income through municipal bond ownership. Municipal bonds are normally sold and traded in minimum denominations of $5,000, an amount too large for many individual investors.

The sponsor of an investment trust assembles a portfolio of securities and sells pieces, or "units," of the trust to investors. Income earned by the trust is passed along to the owners of the trust's units. A trust's owners each receive periodic income payments from the trust in proportion to the number of units that they hold. For example, the owner of ten units of a UIT will receive double the payments received by an investor owning five units of the same UIT. To this point the description of the unit investment trust makes it appear virtually identical to a mutual fund or a closed-end investment company.

A major difference between UITs and investment companies is the extent to which the securities portfolio of an investment trust is managed—it isn't! Mutual funds and closed-end investment companies pay hefty salaries to professional portfolio managers who are expected to use their expertise to trade securities in order to improve shareholders' returns. The portfolio of a unit investment trust does not require continuous management because the portfolio does not change.

How a Unit Investment Trust Is Organized

Suppose a financial services company decides to offer investors partial ownership in a diversified portfolio of municipal bonds. The firm knows that investors are always interested in earning tax-exempt income, a desire that is reinforced by the likelihood that federal income tax rates may soon be increasing. The firm acquires approximately $10 million each of fifteen different municipal bond issues for a total investment of $150 million dollars. The bonds are acquired from other institutional investors in the secondary market (the market in which outstanding securities are traded).

Units of the trust will be sold to investors at a price equal to the total market value of the bonds held in the trust divided by the number of units being sold. For example, if the sponsors decide to organize the trust with 150,000 ownership units, each unit will be sold to investors for approximately $1,000 ($150 million/150,000 units). Units of the trust are sold through sales agents who charge a fee for their service.

The rate at which new trusts are formed depends upon investors' demand for these products. If investors have recently exhibited an interest in high-yield, high-risk junk bonds, sponsors will organize and market new trusts that hold portfolios of these securities. When one trust has been successfully distributed, the sponsor is likely to begin the

> If you own shares in a mutual fund that has all or part of its portfolio invested in U.S. government bonds, don't forget to account for this when you file your state income taxes. Interest income from U.S. government bonds is generally not taxable by state and local authorities.

process all over again, assuming there is sufficient demand from investors. If investors enter a period in which they are concerned about the risks of investing in securities, sponsors are likely to concentrate on organizing new trusts that own portfolios of U.S. government securities or high-grade corporate bonds. Sponsors often organize trusts with portfolios that have a narrow focus. Some trusts concentrate on investments in a certain region of the world or a certain state or region in the United States. For example, unit trusts that own tax-exempt municipal bonds issued in the state of New York are very popular because of the large number of New York residents who are potential customers and the high tax rates faced by residents of that state. Investment trusts holding portfolios of tax-exempt bonds issued in California are also very popular.

Unlike mutual funds and closed-end investment companies that maintain actively managed portfolios, the sponsors of a unit investment trust oversee the portfolio but do not trade or manage the securities held in the portfolio. Basically, the securities that comprise the trust's portfolio at the time the units are first distributed to investors are the securities that will continue to comprise the portfolio. In the case of the municipal bond trust discussed earlier in this chapter, the same municipal bonds will continue to be held until these securities mature or are redeemed prior to maturity.

Bonds deemed to be overvalued are not sold from the trust's portfolio and immediately replaced by other bonds with higher yields, superior risk characteristics, or different maturities. Likewise, the money received from any bond redemptions will be passed along to the owners of the trust's units rather than reinvested. Investors who purchase units of an investment trust that holds a portfolio of bonds will have their original investment gradually returned at the same time they are receiving income from interest payments being made on bonds that remain in the trust's portfolio. Interest income earned by the trust and, as a result, dividends paid to the trust's owners will decline as bonds held by the trust mature.

The schedule by which the bonds in a trust's portfolio will mature or the extent to which the securities will be called depends upon the particular types of bonds a sponsor has selected. Some trusts are organized with portfolios of relatively short-term bonds that mature in five years or less. Other trusts specialize in owning intermediate-length or long-term bonds.

The Value of a Unit Investment Trust

The value of a trust unit depends upon two variables: the value of the assets held in the trust's portfolio and the number of outstanding ownership units of the trust. An investment trust that holds a portfolio with a market value of $100 million and has 100,000 ownership units outstanding will have its units valued at approximately $1,000 each. If the market value of the trust's portfolio increases, there will be a proportionate increase in the value of each of the ownership units. For example, the units of an investment trust that holds a portfolio of long-term bonds will increase in value if interest rates decline. The more interest rates decline, the more the trust's ownership units will increase in value. The investment success of a unit investment trust depends not upon the trading skills of portfolio managers, but rather upon the original portfolio that comprises the trust.

When you purchase investment trust units during the

> Buying shares of a closed-end fund at a discount from net asset value doesn't ensure a profit since you may eventually have to sell the shares at a discount.

original distribution, you are reasonably assured of having all or most of your outlay eventually returned so long as the trusts hold secure investments and so long as you hold the units until the trust is eventually dissolved. If you purchase a trust after the original distribution, or if you unexpectedly need to sell units of a trust, you could receive more or less than you paid because trust ownership units are subject to changing values as the securities held in their portfolios change in value.

Most sponsors of unit investment trusts maintain a secondary market in units of the trusts they originate. The secondary market permits you to sell investment trust units that you have purchased but no longer want. You may also purchase previously issued UITs in the secondary market.

The Costs of Investing in Unit Investment Trusts

UITs don't require a lot of management, but the units do often require a substantial amount of selling effort. The main cost of investing in a unit investment trust is the 2 percent to 5 percent sales fee that is added to the amount of your investment. The sales fee is a one-time charge paid at the time units are purchased. For example, if you invest $10,000 in a unit investment trust that charges a 5 percent sales fee, you will be charged a commission of $500 in addition to the $10,000 principal amount of the purchase.

Sponsors of unit trusts typically establish commission

schedules with sliding fees that depend on the amount of money invested. The sponsor of a trust may charge a commission of 4.5 percent for purchases of up to 200 units, 4 percent for purchases of 201 to 399 units, 3 percent for purchases of 401 to 999 units, and 2 percent for purchases of 1,000 units and over. Trust units purchased in the secondary market (as opposed to units purchased when a trust is initially formed) also carry a sales commission determined by a schedule that may differ somewhat from the commission originally charged on the same units. Trust units that you purchase from the sponsor in the secondary market will have been repurchased by the sponsor from another investor. A trust sponsor attempts to profit from secondary transactions by selling the units at a slightly higher price than it pays to purchase the units and also by charging another sales commission.

CHAPTER 9

Sources of Information about Mutual Funds

There has been an explosion in recent years of financial and investment information of all kinds including reporting on mutual funds. Most people have a limited amount of time to devote to this information and must be able to select the most useful sources. Mutual fund price quotations are available on a daily and weekly basis in many widely available publications. Information on specific mutual funds is provided by several popular periodicals and by a number of specialized publications. Some of these publications are reasonably priced and well worth the investment.

You are most likely to select investments appropriate to your needs when you are an informed investor. To become informed you must know where to obtain specific kinds of investment information. Suppose you are watching a television discussion about investments and several of the participants mention that they believe it is a good time to invest in the petroleum industry. The analysts forecast an increasing demand for petroleum-based products and a resulting increase in oil prices and profits for companies in the industry. You have evaluated your own investment goals and have determined that an investment in the petroleum industry would fit nicely with the other investments you currently own. Rather than purchase shares in a single company, you would like to buy into the portfolio of a mutual fund that holds a diversified portfolio of petroleum stocks. Do any mutual funds specialize in investments in this industry? If so, how can you obtain information about their fees, expenses, and investment track records?

Perhaps you have decided that you would like to increase your current investment income by acquiring shares in a mutual fund that invests in long-term government securities. How can you determine which of these specialized funds have been offering the highest yields and which funds invest only in direct obligations of the government? If you have decided to limit your selection to a no-load fund, how do you go about finding the addresses and phone numbers of sponsors that sell their funds by mail?

The Investment Company Institute, the association of the mutual fund industry, is a good place to begin your search for information about mutual funds. The Institute makes available without charge several excellent publications including *Reading the Mutual Fund Prospectus*. The Institute

> Before you participate in a mutual fund's reinvestment plan, make certain that no fee is charged on shares purchased in the plan. A sales fee on shares purchased with reinvested dividends and capital gains distributions is unfair and should not be tolerated.

also publishes a mutual fund directory that provides addresses, phone numbers, and information on minimum investment requirements and types of fees charged. The directory is available from the Institute for a nominal charge ($8.50 in 1995). The Investment Company Institute may be reached at 1401 H Street, NW, Suite 1200, Washington, DC 20005 (202–293–7700).

Information about Mutual Fund Prices

Mutual fund share values are published daily in most large metropolitan newspapers. *The Wall Street Journal* includes an extensive daily listing of mutual fund prices while most other papers have abbreviated listings both in terms of the number of funds included and the amount of data published for each listing. Mutual fund shareholders can obtain current mutual fund values by calling the appropriate fund, usually via a toll-free number. Some mutual fund sponsors have sophisticated telephone information systems that permit callers using Touch-Tone telephones to enter a series of tones and obtain current prices. *Barron's*, a sister publication of *The Wall Street Journal* that is published each Monday, contains weekly price data that includes each fund's 52-week high and low. It also presents information about recent dividend and capital gains distributions. Mutual fund

Figure 24

MUTUAL FUND PRICE LISTINGS

Fund	NAV	Offer Price	NAV Chg
The Scott Group			
Scott GvmtB	10.30	NL	+.10
Scott Growth	9.95	10.35	−.05
Scott Income	12.20	NL	...
Scott ValueFd	15.00	15.90	+.30

share values are also available via the Internet for investors with computers.

Figure 24 shows mutual fund price listings as they often appear in daily newspapers. The Scott Group is shown as the sponsor of four funds. Entries in the NAV column indicate the net asset value for each fund at the close of trading on the previous trading day. (You will read about Wednesday's trading data in Thursday's newspaper.) For example, the Scott Government Bond Fund has an NAV of $10.30, an amount that is calculated by dividing the number of the fund's outstanding shares into the market value of the fund's portfolio of government bonds. The offer price indicates the price at which the fund was being offered to new investors at the close of trading on the previous day. The "NL" entry means that the Scott Government Bond Fund is a no-load fund that is sold to new investors at the net asset value. Thus, the NAV and the offering price are identical. The

Scott Value Fund is being offered to new investors at $15.90 per share, 90 cents above the fund's net asset value. The 90-cent difference between the net asset value and the offering price is the maximum sales fee per share that will be charged to investors who purchase shares in the fund. Entries under "NAV Chg" are the changes in each mutual fund's net asset value that occurred between the close of trading on this day and the previous trading day. According to the information provided, both the Scott Government Bond Fund and the Scott Value Fund increased in value while the Scott Growth Fund decreased in value. A series of dots or no entry in this column indicates that no change in value occurred between the two trading dates.

Price information for closed-end investment companies is also included in the daily stock quotations of most large daily newspapers. Closed-end price quotations are presented in an identical manner to quotations for other common stocks. Both the closing prices and the respective net changes are included in most listings. A paper with a more detailed listing will include the high price and low price for the day and, perhaps, the high price and low price during the most recent fifty-two weeks. Some newspapers present price quotations for closed-end funds in a special section. These listings sometimes include data both for the net asset value and the stock price of each fund. Price quotations in sections reserved for closed-end funds are frequently presented in a manner similar to that illustrated in Figure 25.

Previous chapters identified net asset value as an important measure of a mutual fund's value. NAV is also of interest to investors in closed-end funds that generally sell at prices different from their respective net asset values. Some investors search for closed-end investment companies that

Figure 25

PRICE QUOTATIONS FOR
CLOSED-END INVESTMENT COMPANIES

Fund	Exchange	NAV	Price	% Difference
Mouseketeer Gvmt Bd	NYSE	13.35	13¾	+ 3.00
Vertigo Income Fd	NYSE	11.14	10½	- 5.75

sell at big discounts to their net asset values. Figure 25 indicates the Mouseketeer Government Bond Fund had a closing price the previous trading day of $13.75 per share at the same time that the shares carried a net asset value of $13.35. Thus, the fund's shares currently sell at a 3 percent premium (represented by +) to the net asset value. The percentage premium is calculated by dividing the difference between the two values by NAV. The listing for the Vertigo Income Fund indicates that the fund's shares closed at a price of $10.50, a 5.75 percent discount from the fund's net asset value.

Information about Specific Mutual Funds

Information about particular investment companies, including their fees, is available from a wide variety of sources. Mutual funds have become such a popular investment that any publication dealing with business matters will generally contain at least modest coverage of mutual funds. Several popular periodicals publish occasional issues that are almost exclusively devoted to mutual funds.

Information from Mutual Funds

Mutual fund sponsors are accustomed to bombarding the public with information regarding their products. Likewise, the sponsors expect huge numbers of requests for information. A sponsor of several different funds will normally offer a summary brochure that briefly describes each of the funds. Once you determine the type of mutual fund you are interested in owning (e.g., growth fund, income fund, or specialized sector fund), don't be bashful about calling or writing numerous sponsors and requesting a prospectus. The mutual fund prospectus is one of the most informative circulars available from any source. Keep in mind when reading information other than the prospectus obtained from a mutual fund sponsor that the firm is attempting to convince you to invest in the funds that it oversees.

Information from Periodicals

Business publications frequently publish articles and financial data about mutual funds. Some periodicals distribute special issues that include information about short-term and long-term returns provided by individual funds. These special editions also generally include data on sales charges and annual expense ratios. *Business Week*, *Consumer Reports*, *Forbes*, *Money*, and *Worth* each offer special editions that have historical data for a large number of mutual funds. These and other publications often include some type of

> Select a mutual fund on the basis of research you do rather than on the basis of a tip you receive from a friend who probably doesn't know any more about investing than you do.

ranking system for mutual funds with similar investment objectives. For example, tax-exempt money market funds may be compared with one another in terms of their fees and returns. *Forbes*, a biweekly publication, grades the investment performance for each of the funds it evaluates on a scale of A to F during bull and bear markets. Publications also sometimes include an "honor roll" or "distinguished group" of funds that have consistently earned unusually high returns for their shareholders. Many of these publications include a telephone number for each fund reviewed.

Popular periodicals are a good source for identifying specific funds in which you may want to invest. For example, if you decide to invest in a mutual fund that has capital growth as an investment objective, use a listing supplied by one of the periodicals to identify a dozen or so funds that you find interesting from the standpoint of historical returns and reasonable fees. At this point you will want to obtain more detailed information about the funds in question. One source of detailed information is the prospectus you can obtain directly from each fund. Advisory services also provide information for a fee.

Mutual Fund Advisory Services

Many advisory and financial information services sell financial data and advice about individual mutual funds. Both the quality and the quantity of the information these firms provide vary substantially. Some advisory firms mail monthly

> Buying mutual fund shares through a broker generally entails greater fees than buying shares directly from a fund.

newsletters while others offer a publication plus access to a telephone "hotline" service. Subscription prices vary as widely as quality, so you should always request a sample of the information before you choose to subscribe.

Value Line Publishing, a firm that is best known for *The Value Line Investment Survey*, also publishes the biweekly *The Value Line Mutual Fund Survey,* which analyzes 2,000 stock and bond funds. Using a format that is nearly identical to the older *Investment Survey*, Value Line provides information on each fund's portfolio holdings, management style, performance, and expenses. A fifteen-year performance graph is provided along with data on dividends, capital gains, portfolio turnover, and total return. The service also ranks each fund on a scale of one to five according to the fund's risk and historical return. Figure 26 illustrates a page from *The Value Line Mutual Fund Survey.*

Investment Companies, published by Arthur Wiesenberger Services, is another widely used mutual fund advisory service. This annual publication contains extensive financial data and descriptive information for approximately 600 mutual funds. The description for each fund includes a short history, investment objective, management style, largest current investments, and historical statistics for the previous eleven years. Wiesenberger also publishes a monthly update on risk and performance statistics and a mutual fund directory. Figure 27 shows a sample page from *Investment Companies.*

Morningstar is probably the best-known purveyor of comprehensive information about mutual funds. This firm issues a biweekly publication that includes one page of descriptive information and financial data for approximately 120 different funds. A total of ten different volumes are

> There is no better investment bargain than a subscription to *The Wall Street Journal.* Of course, you must also set aside time to read this daily newspaper.

published during each twenty-week period (i.e., one volume every other week for twenty weeks), at which point the cycle is repeated. Each biweekly mailing includes an index of all 1,240 funds covered by the service. The write-up for each fund includes information about historical performance, fees, the fund's largest portfolio holdings, a short descriptive analysis, and various services offered by the fund. Morningstar rates each mutual fund on the basis of the fund's risk-adjusted return. Figure 28 illustrates a page from the Morningstar service.

Numerous advisory services publish weekly or monthly newsletters about mutual fund investing. The services generally provide information on fees and historical returns for each fund along with recommendations about which funds to buy and which funds to sell. If you are interested in sampling some of the services, pick up a copy of *Barron's* or some other publication that contains a large number of advertisements from advisory services. Advisory services are generally willing to send sample copies on request.

Information Via Your Computer

The increasing availability and use of personal computers in the home has prompted investment companies to provide mutual fund information for this market. Investors with access to a computer can now obtain mutual fund prices and statistics on diskette, compact disk, and online via a

Figure 26

SAMPLE PAGE FROM
THE VALUE LINE MUTUAL FUND SURVEY

THE VALUE LINE MUTUAL FUND SURVEY

AMCAP FUND AMCPX

PEER GROUP	YIELD	NAV	TNA(Mil)
Growth	0.9%	12.89	2995.7

VALUE LINE

OVERALL RANK	RISK RANK	5-YR RETURN
2	3	10.4%
(Above Avg.)	(Average Risk)	(Annualized)

PAST MARKET CYCLE PERFORMANCE

	Fund	Peer	S&P 500
Bull 10/90 - 5/95	+109.9%	+97.6%	+101.6%
Bear 5/90 - 10/90	-21.9%	-16.9%	-14.7%
Bear 8/87 - 11/87	-26.3%	-28.2%	-29.5%

FUND INFORMATION

Address: *333 S. Hope St., 52nd Fl., Los Angeles, CA 90071*
Distributor: *American Funds Distributors*
Advisor: *Capital Research & Management*

Sub-Advisor: *None*
Shareholders: *212,778*
Fiscal Year-End: *February*

Telephone: *800 421-4120*
Date of Inception: *10/10/66*
Funds in Family: *28*

Min. Initial Invest: *$1,000*
Min. Subsequent Invest: *$50*
Telephone Exchanges: *Yes*
Tel. Redemption: *Yes*

Syst. Withdrawal: *Yes*
Auto. Investing: *Yes*
Last Capital Gain: *5/12/95*
Dividends Paid: *Semiannually*

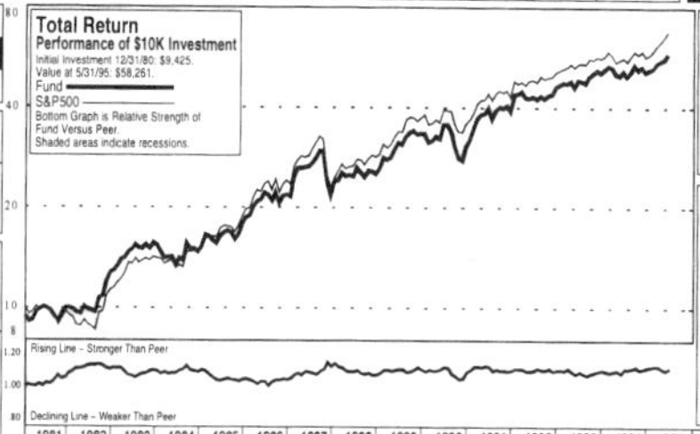

ISSUE DATE

6/27/95

EXPENSE STRUCTURE

Management Fee	0.49%
graded to	0.31%
12b-1 Fee	0.25%
1st Yr. Red. Fee	None
Sales Load	**Pct.**
Maximum	5.75
at $25K	5.75
at $100K	3.50
at $500K	2.00
Minimum	0.00

1981	1982	1983	1984	1985	1986	1987	1988	1989	1990	1991	1992	1993	1994	5/95	HISTORICAL ARRAY
6.08	7.53	8.74	8.27	9.60	9.63	9.81	9.99	11.39	9.97	12.96	13.40	12.83	11.71	12.89	Bid Price (NAV)
0.40	0.17	0.21	0.25	0.19	0.19	0.30	0.29	0.27	0.25	0.15	0.15	0.12	0.13	0.05	Dividends ($)
5.58	2.10	2.26	2.81	1.82	1.65	2.70	2.63	2.06	2.21	1.05	1.03	0.77	0.97	0.91	12-Mo. Div. Yield (%)
0.71	0.09	0.00	0.11	0.24	1.25	0.69	0.39	0.98	0.71	0.46	0.32	1.82	0.95	0.17	Cap. Gains ($)
.82	.82	.77	.73	.69	.54	.51	.63	.70	.72	.79	.75	.73	.72	.71	Expense Ratio (%)
0.89	0.74	0.74	0.65	0.61	0.46	0.40	0.45	0.51	0.53	0.58	0.56	0.59	0.59	0.60	Exp.Ratio Rel. to Peer
43	31	28	15	20	27	17	12	15	18	16	8	15	22	18	Turnover (%)
-	-	712.4	898.0	1126.2	1419.2	1791.6	1690.4	1722.9	1928.1	2204.5	2796.3	3078.8	2877.2	2995.7	Net Assets ($Mil.)
6.2	29.6	19.1	-0.9	22.2	15.5	11.5	8.9	27.1	-4.0	36.9	7.2	11.0	-0.2	12.0	Total Return (%)
11.1	8.2	-3.4	-7.1	-10.0	-3.0	6.3	-7.9	-4.4	-0.8	6.3	-0.6	0.9	-1.6	-5.5	+/- S&P 500 (%)
7.6	3.8	-2.0	0.6	-6.2	0.3	8.8	-5.7	0.9	0.8	1.1	-0.9	-0.5	2.4	-0.6	+/- to Peer (%)
1	2	3	3	5	3	1	4	3	3	3	3	3	2	3	Quintile Perf. Rel. to Peer

PORTFOLIO INFORMATION

SECTOR WEIGHTINGS As of 5/26/95	Port. %	Rel. S&P500
Consumer Durables	0.7	0.18
Energy	0.5	0.05
Finance	15.1	1.22
Industrial Cyclical	8.0	0.49
Non-Durable	18.6	1.20
Retail Trade	1.4	0.23
Health	3.1	0.35
Services	1.9	1.91
Technology	23.4	1.14
Utilities	1.9	0.37

COMPOSITION % As of 3/31/95	
Stock	80
Preferreds	-
Cash	18
Convts.	-
Bonds	2
Other	-
# Stocks	80

STATISTICS

As of 05/26/95	Port. Avg.	% Stock	Rel. S&P 500	Rel. Peer
Price/Earnings	21.41	86	1.16	1.08
Price/Book	4.26	90	1.28	1.32
5-Yr.Earn.Growth %	18.03	76	1.66	1.12
Avg.Mkt.Cap ($Mil.)	13,991	96	0.53	1.28

PORTFOLIO HOLDINGS

Top 20 Equity Holdings As of 2/28/95	VL Rank*	Shares Held	Value ($000)	%Net Assets
TIME WARNER INC	3	3216000	124218	4.18
INTEL CORP	1	1350000	107494	3.62
FEDERAL NATL MTG ASSN	3	1010000	77896	2.62
CAPITAL CITIES ABC INC	2	855000	75667	2.55
COMCAST CORP	-	4685625	73213	2.46
MEDTRONIC INC	1	1200000	72000	2.42
TELE COMMUNICATIONS INC	4	2714000	61744	2.08
GOLDEN WEST FINL CORP DEL	4	1596800	61078	2.06
LOCTITE CORP	3	1295000	59570	2.01
MOTOROLA INC	2	960000	55200	1.86
TELEPHONE & DATA SYS INC	3	1200000	54750	1.84
CELLULAR COMMUNICATIONS PFD CV	-	1095000	54750	1.84
DISNEY WALT CO	2	1000000	53375	1.80
MICROSOFT CORP	2	840000	52815	1.78
FEDERAL EXPRESS CORP	3	765000	49821	1.68
BANC ONE CORP	4	1676188	49238	1.66
PITNEY BOWES INC	4	1375000	48813	1.64
NORWEST CORP	2	1700000	43775	1.47
ORACLE SYS CORP	2	1312500	41016	1.38
WMX TECHNOLOGIES INC	3	1370000	36134	1.22

*Latest available Timeliness ™ rank from Value Line Investment Survey.

PORT. MGR.	%RATING
Team Managed	NR

TAX STATUS 2/28/95	
Unrealized Apprec. %	26

Style/Perf. Quintile

	Value	Growth
Large Cap.		3
Small Cap.		

DIVIDENDS PAID

Year	1st Q	2nd Q	3rd Q	4th Q
1991	0.03	--	--	0.12
1992	--	0.04	--	0.11
1993	--	0.05	--	0.07
1994	--	0.05	--	0.08
1995	--	--	--	--

PERFORMANCE (5/31/95)

	Total Return	+/- % S&P 500	+/- % Peer	Percentile Rank Peer	Value $10,000 Investment	Est. Taxes on $10,000 Investment	Value $10,000 +$100/Mo.
3 MONTHS	6.8	-3.4	-0.8	66	10,063	47	10,260
6 MONTHS	13.2	-5.9	-0.2	58	10,671	50	11,179
1 YEAR	13.3	-6.8	0.8	49	10,680	151	11,823
3 YEAR	10.5	-1.4	0.6	47	12,723	830	16,615
5 YEAR	10.4	-1.1	0.0	51	15,443	1,340	22,900
10 YEAR	13.5	-1.1	0.8	37	33,382	4,678	54,280
15 YEAR	14.7	-0.6	0.5	41	73,900	11,701	122,936
20 YEAR	16.4	2.6	2.4	20	196,812	31,970	329,800

MPT vs. S&P 500

	Fund	Peer
Beta	0.98	0.95
Alpha	-1.0	-1.1
R^2	79	84
Std. Dev.	9.14	8.63

RANKINGS

1 (best) to 5 (worst)		Fund	Peer
Overall		2.9	3.2
Risk		3.3	3.4
Growth	5Yr.	3.4	3.4
Persistence >	1Yr.	2.4	3.0

Recent Developments and Strategies

AMCAP Fund's heavy cash weighting–about 18% at year-end 1994–contributed substantially to its outperformance of its Growth peers last year. Notably, that cash position has not led to a corresponding underperformance so far in 1995, as the fund only modestly lagged its peers through May amid a strong stock-market rally. The fund's competitive performance this year is arguably attributable to its being less-than-fully invested; management will not commit fund assets to investments it is not comfortable with for the sake of full market exposure.

The fund retains a technology bias, a reflection of management's ongoing focus on the information superhighway and other high-tech areas. Time Warner and Intel, at about 4% of assets each, are currently the fund's two largest individual positions.

Management Style

The fund aims for long-term appreciation of capital, primarily by investing in common stocks. The fund may also hold its assets in securities convertible into common stocks, nonconvertible preferred stocks, straight debt securities, U.S. Government securities, and cash equivalents.

AMCAP is led by a management team, a characteristic common to all funds in the American Funds family. The team places emphasis on buying and holding attractively priced securities that have above-average growth prospects, and has the freedom to invest in companies of any size and within any industry. The six "portfolio counselors" each manage a portion of the fund's assets and operate independently, and are compensated based on performance. A team of research analysts acting as a single manager also makes investment decisions. This approach is an attempt to generate consistency of performance and lower volatility relative to funds that employ a single manager. The managers are supported in their efforts by the vast global research arm of Capital Research & Management, the fund's Advisor.

Conclusion

AMCAP Fund currently carries an average Risk rank and an above average Overall rank, an attractive profile for long-term investors seeking growth without the assumption of inordinate short-term volatility.

Figure 27

SAMPLE PAGE FROM WIESENBERGER'S *INVESTMENT COMPANIES*

Fidelity Magellan Fund

Long-Term Growth (LTG)

12/31/93 CDA Rating (1 = lowest, 10 = highest) **6**

Overview

Fidelity Magellan Fund was organized as a diversified open-end investment company in December 1962, and reorganized as a Massachusetts business trust in October 1984. Shares were first offered to the public between 1963 and 1966. Until 1981, the fund made no subsequent public offering of its securities. Shares were issued, however, in payment of distributions when so directed by shareholders. On June 25, 1976, Essex Fund, Inc., was merged into the fund, substantially increasing assets; in June 1981, Salem Fund was also merged. The fund's objective is to seek capital appreciation through investments in securities of both foreign and domestic companies. Normally, the fund's portfolio will be predominantly composed of common stocks or securities convertible into common stock.

Portfolio Characteristics as of 9/93

Largest Holdings	Pct.	Sector Breakdown	Pct.
MOTOROLA INC	2.3	Basic Industries	7.5
TEXAS INSTRS INC	1.6	Cap. Goods & Tech.	27.3
INTEL CORP	1.4	Consumer Cyclicals	18.9
BURLINGTON RES INC	1.4	Consumer Staples	4.8
FORD MTR CO DEL	1.3	Energy	12.3
UNOCAL CORP	1.2	Finance	8.3
CSX CORP	1.2	Transportation	7.6
COLUMBIA HEALTHCARE CORP	1.1	Utilities	9.4
LOWES COS INC	1.1	Miscellaneous	3.8
SEARS ROEBUCK & CO	1.0		
Avg. P/E	27.2	**Market Cap. (mil$)**	6244.6

Administration

Directors: Edward C. Johnson; J. Gary Burkhead; Donald J. Kirk; Richard J. Flynn; E. Bradley Jones; Peter S. Lynch; Edward H. Malone; Gerald C. McDonough; Thomas R. Williams; J. Tyler Wilson; Betram H. Witham; David L. Yunich
Portfolio Manager(s): Jeff Vinik since 1992
Investment Advisor: Fidelity Mgmt & Research Co
Maximum Management Fee (%): 0.820 Graded
Distributor: Fidelity Distributors
Fiscal Year End / Ticker Symbol: May / FMAGX

Shareholder Information

Minimum initial investment: $2,500
Minimum subsequent investment: $250
Max. Front-End Sales Charge: 3.00%
Max. Annual 12b-1 Fee: 1.00
Transfer Agent: Fidelity Service Company
Qualified for Sale: In all states, DC and PR
Address: 82 Devonshire Street; Boston, MA 02109
Telephone: (800) 544-8888; (617) 570-7000

Statistical History

	At Year-End								Annual Data				
					% of Assets in								
Year	Net Assets (mil$)	# of Accounts (000s)	NAV ($)	Yield (%)	Csh Eqv	Bds Pfds	Com Stks	Inc. Divs ($)	Cap. Gains ($)	Exp. Ratio (%)	Total Return	+/-% S&P 500
1993	31,705.1	912.1	70.85	0.9	0	25	75	0.75	6.50	0.99	24.7	14.6
1992	22,268.9	-	63.01	1.7	-	-	-	1.25	8.82	1.64	7.0	-0.6
1991	19,257.1	876.1	68.61	1.7	3	2	95	1.30	5.43	1.06	41.0	10.6
1990	12,325.7	-	53.93	1.4	7	1	92	0.83	2.42	1.03	-4.5	-1.4
1989	12,699.6	892.4	59.85	1.9	11	2	87	1.24	3.82	1.08	34.6	3.0
1988	8,971.1	885.2	48.32	1.8	6	1	93	0.90	0.00	1.14	22.8	6.3
1987	7,800.1	975.1	40.10	1.4	5	0	95	0.72	9.02	1.08	1.0	-4.2
1986	7,405.5	768.3	48.69	0.8	3	2	95	0.46	6.84	1.08	23.7	5.1
1985	4,136.0	430.1	45.21	1.3	1	5	94	0.65	1.78	1.12	43.1	11.4
1984	1,954.6	300.7	33.69	1.0	1	2	97	0.37	3.69	1.04	2.0	-4.1
1983	1,606.9	246.0	37.33	0.6	2	6	92	0.26	1.88	0.85	38.6	16.1
1982	458.4	66.1	28.50	1.1	0	3	97	0.33	1.23	1.34	48.1	26.5

Commenced Operations: 05/26/63

Performance as of 12/31/93

Ann'lzd Total Return	Fund	Avg. LTG	S&P 500
1 Yr.	24.7	11.6	10.1
3 Yr.	23.4	18.0	15.6
5 Yr.	19.3	14.4	14.5
10 Yr.	18.4	12.6	14.9
Bull*	108.6	82.9	68.8
Bear*	-17.2	-17.1	-14.5

MPT Stats.	Fund	Avg. LTG	S&P 500
Alpha	6.03	2.27	-
Beta	1.07	0.98	-
Std Dev	3.47	3.55	3.01

Risk-to-Reward

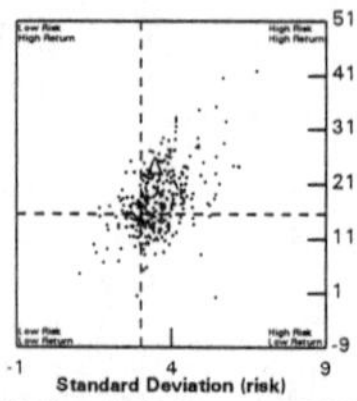

Fd (Δ) vs. all LTG; Intersect: S&P 500

Performance on $10,000 Investment

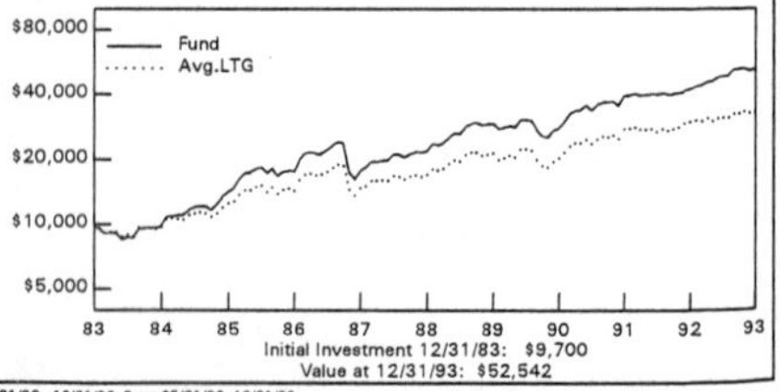

Initial Investment 12/31/83: $9,700
Value at 12/31/93: $52,542

* Returns for most recent market cycle dates are not annualized Bull: 10/31/90 - 12/31/93 Bear: 06/31/90 -10/31/90

Figure 28

SAMPLE PAGE FROM MORNINGSTAR MUTUAL FUND ADVISORY SERVICE

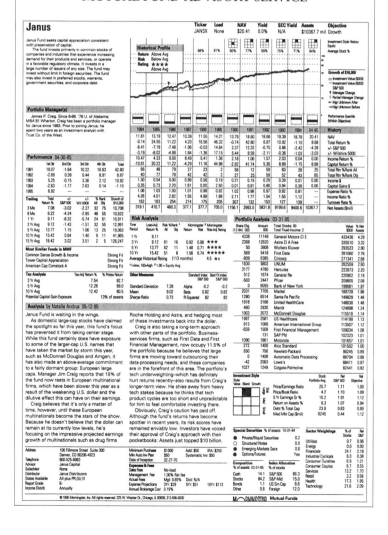

Janus

Ticker	Load	NAV	Yield	SEC Yield	Assets	Objective
JANSX	None	$20.41	0.0%	N/A	$10367.7 mil	Growth

Janus Fund seeks capital appreciation consistent with preservation of capital.

The fund invests primarily in common stocks of companies and industries that experience increasing demand for their products and services, or operate in a favorable regulatory climate. It invests in a large number of issuers of any size. The fund may invest without limit in foreign securities. The fund may also invest in preferred stocks, warrants, government securities, and corporate debt.

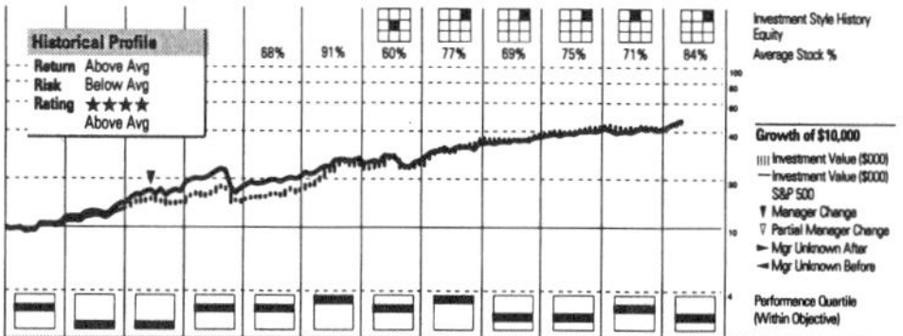

Portfolio Manager(s)

James P. Craig. Since 6-86. '78 U. of Alabama; MBA'81 Wharton. Craig has been a portfolio manager for Janus since 1983. Prior to joining Janus, he spent two years as an investment analyst with Trust Co. of the West.

1984	1985	1986	1987	1988	1989	1990	1991	1992	1993	1994	04-95	History
11.61	13.19	12.47	10.39	11.55	14.21	13.79	18.60	18.68	19.39	18.78	20.41	NAV
-0.14	24.55	11.22	4.20	16.58	46.32	-0.74	42.80	6.87	10.92	-1.10	8.68	Total Return %
-6.41	-7.19	-7.46	-1.06	-0.03	14.64	2.37	12.32	-0.75	0.86	-2.42	-4.28	+/- S&P 500
-3.19	-8.02	-4.88	1.84	-1.36	17.15	5.44	8.59	-2.11	-0.36	-1.03	-3.03	+/- Wilshire 5000
10.47	4.33	0.00	8.49	5.41	1.36	2.18	1.06	1.57	2.03	0.04	0.00	Income Return %
-10.61	20.22	11.22	-4.29	11.16	44.96	-2.92	41.74	5.30	8.89	-1.15	8.68	Capital Return %
66	48	79	27	23	2	58	12	59	60	28	25	Total Rtn %Rank All
40	77	78	42	42	2	27	25	59	52	43	65	Total Rtn %Rank Obj
1.30	0.54	0.00	0.99	0.56	0.19	0.31	0.19	0.29	0.39	0.01	0.00	Income $
0.35	0.73	2.20	1.61	0.00	2.50	0.01	0.91	0.90	0.94	0.39	0.00	Capital Gains $
1.06	1.03	1.00	1.01	0.98	0.92	1.02	0.98	0.97	0.92	0.91	---	Expense Ratio %
4.26	4.01	2.82	1.55	4.99	1.68	2.11	1.77	1.54	1.55	1.12	---	Income Ratio %
162	163	254	214	175	205	307	132	153	127	139	---	Turnover Rate %
319.1	410.7	460.3	377.1	377.7	705.0	1156.1	2993.0	5831.9	9199.6	9400.6	10367.7	Net Assets ($mil)

Performance 04-30-95

	1st Qtr	2nd Qtr	3rd Qtr	4th Qtr	Total
1991	19.07	-1.64	10.22	10.63	42.80
1992	-2.69	0.39	0.44	8.91	6.87
1993	5.25	-0.15	3.36	2.12	10.92
1994	-2.63	-1.17	2.63	0.14	-1.10
1995	6.92	---	---	---	---

Trailing	Total Return %	+/- S&P 500	+/- Wil 5000	% Rank All	% Rank Obj	Growth of $10,000
3 Mo	7.08	-3.02	-2.27	32	75	10,708
6 Mo	6.22	-4.24	-2.85	48	55	10,622
1 Yr	9.11	-8.32	-5.74	24	61	10,911
3 Yr Avg	9.12	-1.43	-1.51	32	55	12,991
5 Yr Avg	13.77	1.15	1.06	13	25	19,063
10 Yr Avg	15.42	0.64	1.40	9	11	41,965
15 Yr Avg	18.42	3.02	3.51	2	5	126,247

Most Similar Funds in MMF

Common Sense Growth & Income	Strong Fit
Tower Capital Appreciation	Strong Fit
American Cap Comstock A	Strong Fit

Tax Analysis	Tax-Adj Return %	% Pretax Return
3 Yr Avg	7.54	82.7
5 Yr Avg	12.26	89.0
10 Yr Avg	12.42	80.5
Potential Capital Gain Exposure		13% of assets

Risk Analysis

Time Period	Load-Adj Return %	Risk %Rank[1] All	Risk %Rank[1] Obj	Morningstar[2] Return	Morningstar[2] Risk	Morningstar Risk-Adj Rating
1 Yr	9.11					
3 Yr	9.12	61	16	0.92	0.66	★★★
5 Yr	13.77	62	11	1.48	0.71	★★★★
10 Yr	15.42	51	8	1.56	0.74	★★★★★
Average Historical Rating	(113 months)					4.5 ★s

[1] 1=low, 100=high [2] 1.00 = Equity Avg

Other Measures			Standard Index S&P 500	Best Fit Index S&P 500
Standard Deviation	7.28	Alpha	-0.2	-0.2
Mean	9.02	Beta	0.82	0.82
Sharpe Ratio	0.73	R-Squared	82	82

Portfolio Analysis 03-31-95

Share Chg (12-94) 000	Amount 000	Total Stocks: 93 / Total Fixed-Income: 2	Value $000	% Net Assets
4336	11149	General Motors Cl E	433436	4.29
2368	12620	Astra Cl A Free	335510	3.32
50	3808	Wolters Kluwer	293523	2.90
569	5418	First Data	281060	2.78
-809	6385	Citicorp	271341	2.68
1630	5802	UNUM	262559	2.60
3177	4780	Hercules	222873	2.20
512	1674	General Re	220902	2.19
-503	2447	Pfizer	209805	2.08
0	6055	Bank of New York	199061	1.97
2031	7705	Mattel	189729	1.88
1280	6514	Santa Fe Pacific	149829	1.48
1918	3166	United HealthCare	148030	1.46
480	2930	Merck	124898	1.24
1003	2072	McDonnell Douglas	115510	1.14
1987	2581	US Healthcare	114199	1.13
913	1089	American International Group	113507	1.12
-659	1509	First Financial Management	109034	1.08
	131	SAP Pfd	102323	1.01
1090	1861	Motorola	101657	1.01
272	1400	Alco Standard	101502	1.00
550	750	Hewlett-Packard	90245	0.89
0	1408	Automatic Data Processing	88704	0.88
-42	2563	Lowe's	88411	0.87
1027	1249	Colgate-Palmolive	82441	0.82

Investment Style

Style: Value Blend Growth; Size: Large Med Small (Blend / Large marked)

	Stock Portfolio Avg	Rel S&P 500	Rel Objective
Price/Earnings Ratio	20.7	1.11	1.00
Price/Book Ratio	4.2	1.10	1.09
5 Yr Earnings Gr %	16.2	1.91	1.12
Return on Assets %	8.3	1.07	0.94
Debt % Total Cap	23.9	0.83	0.89
Med Mkt Cap ($mil)	6245	0.44	1.12

Analysis by Natalie Andrus 05-12-95

Janus Fund is waiting in the wings.

As domestic large-cap stocks have claimed the spotlight so far this year, this fund's focus has prevented it from taking center stage. While this fund certainly does have exposure to some of the larger-cap U.S. names that have taken the market by storm this year, such as McDonnell Douglas and Amgen, it has also made an above-average commitment to a fairly dormant group: European large caps. Manager Jim Craig reports that 19% of the fund now rests in European multinational firms, which have been slower this year as a result of the weakening U.S. dollar and the dilutive effect this can have on their earnings.

Craig believes that it's only a matter of time, however, until these European multinationals become the stars of the show. Because he doesn't believe that the dollar can remain at its currently low levels, he's focusing on the impressive projected earnings growth of multinationals such as drug firms Roche Holding and Astra, and hedging most of these investments back into the dollar.

Craig is also taking a long-term approach with other parts of the portfolio. Business-services firms, such as First Data and First Financial Management, now occupy 11.5% of the portfolio because he believes that large firms are moving toward outsourcing their data-processing needs, and these companies are in the forefront of this area. The portfolio's tech underweighting–which has definitely hurt returns recently–also results from Craig's longer-term view. He shies away from heavy tech stakes because he thinks that tech product cycles are too short and unpredictable for him to feel comfortable investing there.

Obviously, Craig's caution has paid off. Although the fund's returns have become spottier in recent years, its risk scores have remained enviably low. Investors have voiced their approval of Craig's approach with their pocketbooks: Assets just topped $10 billion.

Special Securities	% of assets 10-31-94
● Private/Illiquid Securities	0.2
○ Structured Notes	0.0
● Emerging-Markets Secs	0.6
● Options/Futures	Yes

Composition % of assets 03-31-95		Index Allocation % of stocks	
Cash	14.1	S&P 500	66.3
Stocks	84.2	S&P Mid	15.0
Bonds	1.1	US Sm Cap	6.6
Other	0.6	Foreign	12.0

Sector Weightings	% of Stocks	Rel S&P
Utilities	0.7	0.06
Energy	0.0	0.00
Financials	24.1	2.18
Industrial Cyclicals	6.3	0.38
Consumer Durables	6.9	1.21
Consumer Staples	6.7	0.55
Services	13.2	1.70
Retail	3.2	0.58
Health	17.3	1.95
Technology	21.6	2.09

Address	100 Fillmore Street Suite 300, Denver, CO 80206-4923
Telephone	800-525-8983
Advisor	Janus Capital
Subadvisor	None
Distributor	Janus Distributors
States Available	All plus PR,GU,VI
Report Grade	B-
Income Distrib	Annually

Minimum Purchase	$1000	Add: $50	IRA: $250
Min Auto Inv Plan	$50	Systematic Inv: $50	
Date of Inception	02-27-70		
Expenses & Fees			
Sales Fees	No-load		
Management Fee	1.00% flat fee		
Actual Fees	Mgt: 0.65%	Dist: N/A	
Expense Projections	3Yr: $29	5Yr: $51	10Yr: $113
Annual Brokerage Cost	0.19%		

MORNINGSTAR Mutual Funds

Figure 29

SOURCES FOR MUTUAL FUND SOFTWARE AND ONLINE INFORMATION

The Quarterly Mutual Fund Update
American Association of Individual Investors
312-280-0170
$39 members, $50 non-members
Allows screening of 900 low-load and no-load funds from quarterly data provided on disk.

Value Line Fund Analyzer
212-907-1803
$295 annually with monthly updates
Allows sorting of funds according to 100 criteria. Available on CD-ROM or floppy.

Monacle
Manhattan Analytics, Inc.
800-251-3863
$149; $240 daily data updates; $75 quarterly data updates; $10.95 30-day trial
Daily online service with daily updates for 1,000 funds. Extra service ($99) provides weekly pricing for 2,500 funds.

Mutual Fund Expert
Steele Systems, Inc.
800-237-8400
$95 quarterly subscription; $185 monthly subscription; $45 single issue
Extensive data and tools for screening 7,000 funds on floppy disk.

Mutual Funds OnDisc
Mutual Funds OnFloppy
Closed-End Funds OnFloppy
Morningstar, Inc.
800-876-5005
OnDisc $795 monthly, $495 quarterly, $295 one-time; OnFloppy or Closed-End OnFloppy $195 monthly, $95 quarterly, $45 one-time
Screen 5,700 funds with 700 statistics and 18 years of data with OnDisc; Same funds with 94 statistics and 10 years of data with OnFloppy; Screen 520 funds with 111 statistics and 10 years of data with Closed-End Funds OnFloppy.

modem. Information accessed on a diskette or compact disk often involves a time lag of several weeks or months. Data from an online service is generally current.

Mutual fund information on diskettes generally consists of statistics on expense ratios, sales charges, short-term performance, long-term performance, and volatility. For example, you might want to specify that the program identify all mutual funds in the database that have less than a 1 percent management fee, more than a 10 percent annual return, no sales fee, and low price volatility. Several companies sell this information, although the price and number of funds covered can vary significantly from one service to the next. Be certain to obtain information from several companies so you can compare the cost and the data that is provided.

While online mutual fund information is much more current, it is also likely to be more expensive than information distributed via diskette. Because online services typically charge a connection fee, the expense you incur depends primarily on the amount of time you spend online. Online firms provide mutual fund data that are generally updated on a daily basis. You can use the downloaded data to select and time the purchase and sale of mutual funds included in the database. Online mutual fund information and share prices are also available at several sites via the Internet's World Wide Web.

Glossary

Adviser An individual or organization that provides a mutual fund with investment advice.

Asset Something of monetary value that is owned by a firm or by an individual.

Asset allocation Distributing monies among several investments in some predetermined ratio.

Automatic reinvestment Automatic purchase of additional shares of a mutual fund with dividends and/or capital gains distributions.

Balanced fund A mutual fund with a portfolio that includes both bonds and stocks.

Beat the averages To manage a portfolio so as to earn a return superior to the return calculated on stock market averages such as the Standard & Poor's 500 Index.

Bid The price offered for an asset.

Bond rating The credit quality of a bond as judged by one of the major credit rating agencies.

Break point The amount of money that must be invested in a mutual fund before the sales charge is reduced.

Broker-dealer A firm that buys stock for and sells stock from its own portfolio and that also brings together buyers and sellers of a stock.

Buy-and-hold strategy To purchase a security and hold it for a long period of time.

Capital appreciation An increase in the net asset value of a mutual fund's shares.

Capital gains distribution A payment of realized capital gains by an investment company to its shareholders.

Check-writing privilege The privilege extended to a mutual fund shareholder of being able to write checks against the value of shares held by the investor.

Clone fund A mutual fund with a portfolio that is designed to emulate the portfolio of a different mutual fund.

Closed-end investment company An investment company that has a specific number of authorized shares. The shares are traded in the secondary market among investors.

Contingent deferred sales charge The fee levied by mutual funds on shareholder redemptions when shares have been held less than a specific length of time.

Contractual plan A plan in which a mutual fund shareholder agrees to invest a predetermined amount of money in additional shares of the fund.

Custodian An organization that retains custody of a mutual fund's assets.

Direct marketing The sale of mutual fund shares directly to investors without the assistance of a salesperson.

Discount brokerage firm A brokerage firm that discounts the commissions it charges customers to trade securities.

Diversification Purchasing assets that have returns that are not directly related. Diversification reduces the risk of investing.

Dollar-cost averaging Investing equal amounts of money at periodic intervals.

Double-exempt fund An investment company that invests in the bonds of a specific state and pays dividends that are exempt both from federal and state income taxes.

Ex-distribution Pertaining to mutual fund shares that trade without the right to a specific distribution.

Ex-dividend Pertaining to mutual fund shares that trade without the right to a specific dividend.

Expense ratio An investment company's annual management fee and operating expenses as a percentage of the firm's assets.

Family of funds A group of mutual funds operated by the same sponsor.

Fully invested Pertaining to a mutual fund that has used all of its cash balances to purchase securities.

Fund of funds A mutual fund that purchases the shares of other mutual funds.

Fund switching Selling shares in one mutual fund and using the proceeds to purchase shares in a different mutual fund.

Ginnie Mae fund A mutual fund that invests in obligations guaranteed by the Government National Mortgage Association and passes through to shareholders the interest and principal payments received by the fund.

Growth fund A mutual fund that selects investments that are expected to increase in value.

Income fund A mutual fund that selects investments that will provide current income to the fund's shareholders.

Index fund A mutual fund that maintains a portfolio of securities designed to match the performance of the market as a whole.

Investment banker A company that assists organizations in raising money in the capital markets.

Investment company A company that pools the funds of investors and purchases securities appropriate to the company's investment objectives.

Investment objective The investment goal pursued by a mutual fund.

Junk bond A bond of low credit quality that subjects owners to substantial risk that interest and/or principal payments may not occur as scheduled.

Liquidity A measure of an asset's or pool of assets' ability to be easily converted into cash without affecting the market value.

Load The fee charged to investors who purchase shares in a mutual fund. Also called *sales charge.*

Low-load fund A mutual fund with a sales charge equal to 3 percent or less of the amount of money invested in shares of the fund.

Management fee The payment of a mutual fund to its investment advisers.

Money market fund A mutual fund that uses proceeds from the sale of its shares to acquire high-quality short-term debt securities.

Municipal bond The bond issue of a city, county, state, or other political entity. Interest received from these securities is generally free of federal income taxes.

Mutual fund custodian The organization entrusted with a mutual fund's securities.

National Association of Securities Dealers (NASD) An organization of brokers and dealers that establishes legal and ethical standards for its members.

Net asset value (NAV) The market value of a mutual fund's assets divided by the number of the fund's shares that are outstanding.

Net change The amount by which the closing price of a mutual fund is different from the closing price on the previous trading day.

No-load fund A mutual fund that sells its shares without a sales charge.

Offering price The price at which a mutual fund's shares are sold to investors.

Open-end investment company An investment company that continuously stands ready to redeem its own shares of stock. These firms are commonly referred to as *mutual funds*.

Over-the-counter market (OTC) A widespread web of dealers who make markets in many different securities.

Portfolio A collection of assets.

Portfolio manager An investment specialist who invests and manages a pool of assets.

Portfolio turnover The degree to which a portfolio's assets are subject to trading activity.

Primary market 1. The market in which new securities are sold. Also see *Secondary market*. 2. The market in which most of a security's trading activity occurs.

Prospectus A legal document provided to investors by a firm that is distributing securities. A prospectus includes information about the issuer that investors will need in order to make an informed decision about whether or not to purchase the securities.

Rating See *Bond rating*.

Rating agency A company that grades the credit quality of debt securities.

Regulated investment company An investment company that meets federal regulations that allow it to escape taxation on dividends and realized capital gains that are passed through to the investment company's shareholders.

Reinvestment privilege The privilege of a mutual fund's shareholders to automatically reinvest dividends and capital gains distributions in additional shares of the fund's stock.

Risk The degree of probability of loss on the rate of return an investment will provide.

Sales charge See *Load*.

Secondary market The market in which outstanding securities are traded among investors.

Sector fund A mutual fund that concentrates its portfolio holdings on securities of a restricted nature. For example, a sector fund may invest only in the securities of companies engaged in the health care industry.

Securities and Exchange Commission (SEC) The federal

agency that regulates the securities industry including mutual funds.

Tax-exempt money market fund A mutual fund that invests in short-term tax-exempt debt instruments and that pays federally tax-exempt dividends to shareholders.

Telephone switching Selling shares in a mutual fund and using the proceeds to purchase shares in a different mutual fund via the telephone.

Total return With regard to mutual fund shares, the sum of returns earned from dividends, capital gains distributions, and price appreciation.

Transfer agent The organization that maintains records of a mutual fund's shareholders.

Trustee A person or organization that manages the assets of some other person or organization.

Turnover rate The number of shares traded by an investment company as a percentage of the firm's total portfolio.

12b-1 fee A charge against assets levied by mutual funds to help pay for marketing expenses. This fee reduces the return earned by a mutual fund's shareholders.

Underwriter A firm that distributes shares for a mutual fund.

Unit investment trust An unmanaged portfolio of investments with ownership units that are sold to investors.

Unrealized gain The amount by which an owned asset's current value is greater than the asset's cost.

Unrealized loss The amount by which an owned asset's current value is less than the asset's cost.

Window dressing Changes in a mutual fund's portfolio to create the impression of successful investment choices. Mutual funds sometimes engage in window dressing prior to issuing a financial statement.

Withdrawal plan An option of mutual funds that permits shareholders to sell shares in order to receive specified payments at regular intervals.

Index

About the Author

David L. Scott is Professor of Accounting and Finance at Valdosta State University, Valdosta, Georgia. He was born in Rushville, Indiana, and received degrees from Purdue University and Florida State University before earning a Ph.D. in economics at the University of Arkansas at Fayetteville.

Professor Scott has authored two dozen books on personal finance and investing, including eight other titles in the Money Smarts series, *How Wall Street Works* (Irwin Professional Publishing), and *Wall Street Words* (Houghton Mifflin). He regularly conducts workshops on topics related to investing and personal finance.

Dr. Scott and his wife, Kay, are the authors of the two-volume *Guide to the National Park Areas* published by the Globe Pequot Press. They spend their summers traveling throughout the United States and Canada in their fourth Volkswagen camper.